Stratification and Inequality Series
The Center for the Study of Social Stratification and Inequality,
Global COE Program
Tohoku University, Japan
Volume 13

Social Exclusion

Stratification and Inequality Series

The Center for the Study of Social Stratification and Inequality,
Global COE Program
Tohoku University, Japan

Inequality amid Affluence: Social Stratification in Japan
Junsuke Hara and Kazuo Seiyama

Intentional Social Change: A Rational Choice Theory
Yoshimichi Sato

Constructing Civil Society in Japan: Voices of Environmental Movements
Koichi Hasegawa

Deciphering Stratification and Inequality: Japan and beyond
Yoshimichi Sato

Social Justice in Japan: Concepts, Theories and Paradigms
Ken-ichi Ohbuchi

Gender and Career in Japan
Atsuko Suzuki

Status and Stratification:
Cultural Forms in East and Southeast Asia
Mitsuhiko Shima

Globalization, Minorities and Civil Society:
Perspectives from Asian and Western Cities
Koichi Hasegawa and Naoki Yoshihara

Fluidity of Place: Globalization and the Transformation of Urban Space
Naoki Yoshihara

Japan's New Inequality: Intersection of
Employment Reforms and Welfare Arrangements
Yoshimichi Sato and Jun Imai

Minorities and Diversity
Kunihiro Kimura

Inequality, Discrimination and Conflict in Japan:
Ways to Social Justice and Cooperation
Ken-ichi Ohbuchi and Nobuko Asai

Social Exclusion: Perspectives from France and Japan
Marc Humbert and Yoshimichi Sato

Series Editor: Yoshimichi Sato, Tohoku University

Editorial Board: Koichi Hasegawa, Ken-ichi Ohbuchi, Toshiaki Kimura, Ichiro Numazaki, Yoshimichi Sato, Masahiro Tsujimoto, Mary C. Brinton, Jeffrey P. Broadbent

Stratification and Inequality Series
The Center for the Study of Social Stratification and Inequality,
Global COE Program
Tohoku University, Japan
Volume 13

Social Exclusion

Perspectives from France and Japan

Edited by

Marc Humbert

and

Yoshimichi Sato

First published in 2012 by
Trans Pacific Press, PO Box 164, Balwyn North, Victoria 3104, Australia
Telephone: +61 (0)3 9859 1112 Fax: +61 (0)3 8911 7989
Email: tpp.mail@gmail.com
Web: http://www.transpacificpress.com

Copyright © Trans Pacific Press 2012

Designed and set by Digital Environs, Melbourne, Australia. www.digitalenvirons.com

Printed by BPA Print Group, Burwood, Victoria, Australia

Distributors

Australia and New Zealand
DA Information Services/Central Book Services
648 Whitehorse Road
Mitcham, Victoria 3132
Australia
Telephone: +61-3-9210-7777
Fax: + 61-3-9210-7788
Email: books@dadirect.com
Web: www.dadirect.com

USA and Canada
International Specialized Book Services (ISBS)
920 NE 58th Avenue, Suite 300
Portland, Oregon 97213-3786
USA
Telephone: 1-800-944-6190
Fax: 1-503-280-8832
Email: orders@isbs.com
Web: http://www.isbs.com

Asia and the Pacific
Kinokuniya Company Ltd.

Head office:
3-7-10 Shimomeguro
Meguro-ku
Tokyo 153-8504
Japan
Telephone: +81-3-6910-0531
Fax: +81-3-6420-1362
Email: bkimp@kinokuniya.co.jp
Web: www.kinokuniya.co.jp

Asia-Pacific office:
Kinokuniya Book Stores of Singapore Pte., Ltd.
391B Orchard Road #13-06/07/08
Ngee Ann City Tower B
Singapore 238874
Telephone: +65-6276-5558
Fax: +65-6276-5570
Email: SSO@kinokuniya.co.jp

All rights reserved. No production of any part of this book may take place without the written permission of Trans Pacific Press.

ISBN 978-1-920901-69-1 (Paperback)

Contents

Figures	vi
Tables	vii
List of Contributors	viii
Preface *Marc Humbert and Yoshimichi Sato*	x

1. Equality of Places vs. Equality of Opportunities *François Dubet* — 1
2. Stability and Increasing Fluidity in the Contemporary Japanese Social Stratification System *Yoshimichi Sato* — 8
3. The Paradoxa of Exclusion: Crossed Considerations on the Contemporary Forms of Broken Social Links *Serge Paugam* — 20
4. Poverty and Exclusion in Japan: Young People and their Hopes *Yûji Genda* — 32
5. The Insertion of Young People into the Labor Market, and Job Quality *François-Xavier Devetter* — 44
6. Changes and Problems in the Youth Labor Market in Japan *Yuki Honda* — 62
7. Policies against Social Exclusion in France *Xavier Emmanuelli* — 75
8. Public Policies toward Homeless and the Politicization of Civil Society in Japan *David-Antoine Malinas* — 86
9. Comparison of Poor People's Participation in Social Movements in France and Japan *Nanako Inaba* — 102
10. Employment at All Costs? Limits and Shortfalls of French Employment Policies *Pierre Concialdi* — 116
11. When Law is Facing Poverty: Looking for a New "Adjudicative Space" for Social Rights *Isabelle Giraudou* — 129

Notes	144
Bibliography	151
Index	159

List of Figures

2.1: The effect of company size on duration of first job   12
2.2: Proportions of female regular/non-regular workers by education and birth cohort   13
2.3: Proportion of job changes resulting in income reduction across educational strata and over time   15
5.1: The situation of young people three years after finishing their initial education   49
5.2: Proportion of employees based on total number of constraints   54
5.3: The proportion of employees declaring that their work is very often, or often, monotonous   55
6.1: Change in the number of young people (aged 15–34)   64
6.2: Distribution of annual income (age total)   65
6.3: Rate of male regular workers who work more than 60 hours per week (according to age)   66
6.4: Number of claims for workers' compensation insurance according to the type of illness   67
6.5: Shift in the rate of workers in the manufacturing industry (by country)   70
6.6: Number of youth who feel that they have acquired vocational skills through education (according to educational background)   71
6.7: Model of "flexpeciality"   72
6.8: Envisaged model of youth labor market   73
7.1: Risk-related apportionment of social protection services offered (2004)   77
8.1: Social inclusion policy—Support Center for Homeless Autonomy   99

List of Tables

3.1: Definition of the different types of link according to the forms of protection and of recognition	27
3.2: Broken social links	28
5.1: Proportion of employees and manual workers subject to each type of constraint according to age	56
5A1: The parameters and thresholds used to build the indicator	58
10.1: Main characteristics of employment policies	119
10.2: Percentage of the labor force that is either on a low wage job or unemployed during three years	125

List of Contributors

Pierre Concialdi
IRES, Institut de recherches économiques et sociales, Paris.

François-Xavier Devetter
Clersé- CNRS, Télécom-Lille 1.

François Dubet
EHESS, Université Bordeaux Segalen, CNRS, UMR 5116 Centre Emile Durkheim.

Xavier Emmanuelli
Samusocial International, Paris.

Yūji Genda
Institute of Social Science, The University of Tokyo.

Isabelle Giraudou
French Research Institute on Contemporary Japan (CNRS-MAEE), Tokyo, Associate Researcher at Lyon Institute of East Asian Studies (CNRS, UMR 5062).

Yuki Honda
Graduate School of Education, The University of Tokyo.

Marc Humbert
CNRS, University of Rennes, French Research Institute on Contemporary Japan, Tokyo.

Nanako Inaba
College of Humanities, Ibaraki University.

David-Antoine Malinas
Institut Français de Recherche à l'Étranger UMIFRE 19 CNRS-MAE, International Advanced Research and Education Organization, Tohoku University, and Center for the Study of Social Stratification and Inequality, Tohoku University.

Serge Paugam
EHESS, CNRS, ERIS (Equipe de Recherche sur les Inégalités Sociales), Centre Maurice Halbwachs, Paris.

Yoshimichi Sato
Graduate School of Arts and Letters, Tohoku University.

Preface

Marc Humbert and Yoshimichi Sato

Within a few decades, the global dream of building a "middle class society" has vanished almost everywhere, giving way to an emerging global nightmare: "Social Exclusion". France and Japan had been among the most successful societies, taken as examples by the rest of the world that it is indeed possible for a nation to include (almost) an entire population in the middle class. However, even these two countries have suffered increasing disillusion since the 1980s. The main concern of these countries now is social exclusion, and the aim of this book is to document and contrast the French and Japanese situations as well as French and Japanese analyses of social exclusion. Of course, the authors of this book are not merely objective scientific observers; they are also citizens who share the idea that it would be better to avoid social exclusion and seek a path that might lead to a society without social exclusion.[1]

With general agreement that social exclusion has been increasing for decades and has now become widespread, it would seem at first sight to be an easy task to organize an international symposium and a collective publication such as this one. However, to document the phenomenon precisely, get an accurate measure of it, list its main features, assess the trend of its evolution and identify measures that might curb this trend requires the use of a wide array of methodologies; and the use of a wide array of methodologies generates fairly diverse appreciations of the phenomenon in question.

This confrontation of authors, analyses and different situations has been very stimulating. A brief account of what we mean by that must begin with a discussion of the signification of the two keywords of this book: "social" and "exclusion".

The link between the term "social" and "economic" seems almost unavoidable. In fact, the main use of the word "social" is to invoke the hypothesis that society is not a homogenous entity and that its heterogeneity rests upon economic differences—differences in income—between individuals (or groups of individuals). These differences are read as inequalities. When these inequalities leave lower income individuals feeling as if they have fallen into a poverty trap, society is faced with a situation of exclusion. This approach assumes that this exclusion is an economic issue: it is a problem of income distribution, where exclusion is exclusion of the poor from fair access to products and services. Although the economy is not the only factor contributing to social exclusion, all chapters refer to it, and most often they refer to the situation of individuals (or groups of individuals) who could fall into a situation of exclusion. One key factor is the possibility of being employed and receiving a sufficient income to avoid this threat.

On this point, the French and Japanese situations are in many respects quite similar and in other respects they are quite different. All of our authors, whether French or Japanese, agree that the best way for society to avoid this failure, which relegates some part of its membership to a situation of exclusion, is the one in which both France and Japan excelled for many years: to ensure a high performing education system, at all levels, to prepare young people to undertake economic activity with deep commitment and to develop the aspiration to join the middle class society. However this is no longer the case in either country. As Sato documents in Chap. 2, some groups are set aside in contemporary society; most obvious are poorly educated young people, but also older people, migrants and women, none of whom are so thoroughly embedded in the work place as the educated male permanent workers aged 35–55. The importance of the young to changing the trend of increasing levels of social exclusion is evident from the number of chapters which address the issues that they are facing (Genda, Chap. 4; Devetter, Chap. 5; Honda, Chap. 6).

One of the more significant differences between the French and Japanese is clearly visible in the attitudes towards homeless people, who are by definition poor and socially excluded. In France social movements tackling homelessness help people to get housing while their counterparts in Japan mainly seek to get homeless people a job (See Malinas, Chap. 8; Inaba, Chap. 9). This difference is discussed in this book (especially by Inaba, Chap.9), but a fully satisfactory explanation of it is still a matter for further research.

The role of the welfare state has been ingrained in the minds of the people of France, including the role of the law to deliver justiciable "rights" (see Giraudou, Chap. 11) and the necessity of policies to lift the poor out of poverty. In France unemployment is a major problem, but it is considered to be the responsibility of the State to give all of her citizens, whether unemployed or not, what they need to live with dignity: including unemployment benefits, minimum wages, housing allowances, etc. Somehow the fight against unemployment (Concialdi, Chap. 10) and the fight against social exclusion (Emmanuelli, Chap. 7) have been separated in France. Or rather, they "were" separated. As the chapters of this book make clear, things have changed significantly over the past two or three decades with the extension of the exclusion phenomenon.

In Japan social inclusion was for many decades secured by long-term employment, permanent employment and by other forms of employment to ensure that the general rate of unemployment was kept extremely low compared to other countries (especially France), and thus there was no need for specific public policies targeting unemployment. In other words, in Japan, social inclusion did not come from the welfare state—at least in its component of access to individual consumption through income and money—but from private and public sector employers. Here, again, things have changed.

One fundamental change that has occurred in this regard is raised by the later evolution of social exclusion, which has resulted in a clear duality in these societies. The theoretical case for this duality is argued by Dubet in Chap. 1 and is statistically substantiated by Sato in Chap. 2. As Paugam makes clear in Chap. 3, the way out of the present situation can only be found by considering the core characteristics of society which is not economic—made of incomes and expenses—but sociological—made of relationships and symbols.

Dubet discusses the fundamental tension between the quest for equality of places and equality of opportunities. Sato, examining the evolution of social stratification, differentiates two social phenomena, stability and fluidity. To some extent, we can correlate equality of places with stability, and equality of opportunities with fluidity. The authors in this book avoid the Marxian conception of social class along with all of its heavily laden rhetoric. Instead, we focus on "places" and "strata". It is clear, then, that equality of places and stability was the principal concern in any "real" middle class society: income differences (which were much less than in the past) existed between individuals according to their different places; these individuals belonged to different strata but the fact of different places and strata was not evidence of an unequal society. Income differences were understood to be justified by the differences in the services delivered to society by the corresponding individuals. The education system ensured entry to the system of places and strata at a certain level, and then the labor market and welfare state / enterprise system provided some fluidity of opportunity within the frame of a middle class society.

Over the past two or three decades, erosion of the enterprise system and of the welfare state has led to a new structure of places and strata. Differences in income and opportunities have been extended up to such an extent that they are now felt to be unequal and unjustified. Relying mainly on contributions based upon mainstream economics the main response of politicians to this situation has been to advocate the promotion of equality of opportunities or fluidity: to extend meritocracy after the exit of the education system, to replace the enterprise system (of full-time, permanent employment) with an external (casualized, precarious) labor market and/or self-employment, to replace the welfare state system with greater labor market flexibility. The outcome in both countries has been even more social exclusion.

The chapters in this book show that this evolution is jeopardizing our societies, hurting them at their core. The "remedies" proposed by the politicians for this issue focus on economic dimensions, while it is the sociological dimensions that are at stake. Several chapters of this book show precisely this, through analyses of specific case studies of youth and homeless people (especially, chapters 4–9). Although there is no specific discussion of the plight of women in this volume, we maintain that any such analysis would reach the same conclusions. In most cases of "exclusion", an unemployed person does not view employment merely as a source of income. Nor does s/he see consumption mainly as access to merchandise that matches material needs. Rather, income and consumption are seen principally as a means to be included in the society, to be recognized for his or her value by others, by society, to be like others. Paugam (Chap. 3) puts this quite clearly, reminding us of Durkheim's distinction: individuals do not only *count on* mechanical solidarity, but, above all, are keen to *count for* others and for the organic solidarity of society. But the sheer reality of recent decades is that mechanical solidarity and, what is worse, organic solidarity are both endangered.

Each chapter in this book is an independent and self-contained discussion of its specific subject such that the reader can learn of any one of these topics with no need to read the others. However the chapters have been presented in a specific order. The first three chapters (Dubet, Sato, Paugam) address the general issue of social exclusion whereas the remaining chapters are each dedicated to specific themes and specific contrasts between the French and

Japanese situations, all of which contribute to a broad understanding of this phenomenon. Young people are at the center of chapters 4 (Genda), 5 (Devetter) and 6 (Honda). Then the book turns to examine the cases of homeless people (chapters 7, Emmanuelli, 8, Malinas and 9, Inaba). These three chapters focus on social movements although chapters 7 and 8 also deal with questions of public intervention, which is also the theme of chapter 10 (Concialdi), which analyzes French employment policies. The final chapter (Giraudou) is also centered on France where—together with international attempts—some of the rights expressed in international or national charts or agreement come to be "justiciable". A justiciable right means that someone who cannot access a specific right can sue in court to get it from the State. Utopia? It is difficult to say that this view of justiciable right is realistic, and we are not convinced that the law alone could ever suffice to eliminate social exclusion. But is there any good society without a good set of rules, a good law? That is perhaps another debate. The question here is: is it possible to build a society without exclusion? We hope that this book will help the reader to reach a conclusion about this.

Acknowledgements

We gratefully thank the French Research Institute on Contemporary Japan and the Center for the Study of Social Stratification and Inequality of Tohoku University for their academic and financial support for this book project. We also thank Airin Izumi, Fukuo Ootomo, and Miho Kimura for their incredibly proficient secretarial work at the Center. We cannot forget the efficient support from the team of *Nichifutsukaikan* (Tokyo) that hosted the conference where we held a stimulating French-Japanese debate. Last but not least, we are profoundly grateful to Professor Yoshio Sugimoto of Trans Pacific Press for his marvelous editorial support.

1 Equality of Places vs. Equality of Opportunities

François Dubet

Social justice can be characterized today by the combination, the juxtaposition and the opposition of two major conceptions, although their definition and the tensions between them are often masked by inspirationally generous principles and vague terminology. Both of these conceptions of social justice aim to resolve the same issue: they seek to reduce the fundamental tension in democratic societies between claiming the fundamental equality of all individuals, on the one hand, and the actual social inequalities stemming from traditions, competing interests and the "normal" operation of modern societies, on the other. Both of these major solutions include the equality of *places* and the equality of *opportunities*. In both cases, the idea is to reduce certain social inequalities so as to make them acceptable, if not perfectly fair, in the society in which we are living.

Obviously, both of these conceptions of social justice are excellent: everybody most likely wishes to live in a society both relatively equalitarian and relatively meritocratic. We are also scandalized by income discrepancies between the poorest and those who receive a few dozen years of minimum wages per annum, and by the discriminations imposed upon minorities, women and the various segregated groups who cannot hope to change social position because they are seemingly anchored in their appropriate stations. At first view, the choice between the model of places in society and the model of opportunities is all the more restricted, judging by Rawls and many others before him, since a truly just democratic society must necessarily combine the fundamental equality of all its members and the "just inequalities" derived from fair meritocratic competition. We know all too well that such chemistry lies at the heart of a democratic and liberal political philosophy which secures everyone the right to run his/her life as he/she wishes within common law and "contract".

Equality of places in society

The first of these conceptions of social justice is centered on the *places* organizing social structure, that is to say all the positions occupied by individuals, regardless whether men or women, members of visible minorities or of the "white" majority, "educated" or not so "educated", young or elderly people, etc. This representation of social justice leads to reduce inequalities in income, life conditions, access to services, safety, etc, which are associated with the social positions occupied by quite different individuals in numerous aspects: qualifications, sex, age, skills and so on. The equality of places seeks to tighten the structure of social positions without emphasis on individuals moving round various unequal places. Here, social mobility is an indirect consequence of relative social equality. In one word, the idea is not so much to promise workers' children that they stand as many chances of becoming executives as executives' children, as to reduce the discrepancy between workers and executives as regards their life and work conditions. The aim is not so much to enable women to occupy on a par the jobs today reserved to men as to see to it that the jobs filled by women and by men are as equal as possible.

The equality of places has been supported by the labor movement and, more widely speaking, left-wing parties. For more than a century, the labor movement has sought to reduce inequalities between social positions thanks to social health insurance against life accidents and economy fluctuations, by the redistribution of wealth through social deductions and gradual income tax and, by the development of public service and the Welfare State. Social inequalities are formed or reduced first and foremost in work conditions and in wages. At the end of the day, the countries which have developed such policies are significantly less inegalitarian than the others. Strikingly, the social justice model has built a representation of society in terms of social classes and work inequality indices. But beyond that, the equality of places builds an extended social contract and a solidarity largely "blind" to "debts", "receivables" and each individual's liabilities.

But this model of justice today is subject to numerous criticisms. It is reproached for having developed a corporatist State in which everyone defends his position and the advantages he has acquired. In this sense, it would be inefficient; for example, liberal criticism relentlessly points out the high unemployment rates of corporatist Welfare States. It is also reproached with weakening social confidence and cohesion since everyone needs assistance from the State rather than from other bodies. The equality of places is often deemed to be conservative. Blind to the discrimination inflicted to women and workers especially, white educated men appear to be privileged; everyone would hence be invited to remain in his or her station rather than changing it. Finally, the equality of places would be increasingly difficult to stand by in a globalised world where social protection systems are competing.

Equality of opportunities

The second conception of justice, now gradually getting the upper hand, is centered on the equality of opportunities offered to all of occupying any place according to a meritocratic principle. Its aim is not so much to reduce inequality in social positions as to fight against discriminations whereby everyone should rely on his own merits so as to reach unequal positions after fair competition wherein equal individuals compete against each other to fill hierarchized social places. In such a case, inequalities are fair since all places are open to all. With the equality of opportunities, the definition of social inequalities substantially changes with respect to the model of places since the latter refers less to position inequalities than to all of the obstacles to the formation of fair competition, without questioning the structure of the places a priori. Here, the ideal is not that of a society wherein position inequalities would be limited; it is that of a society wherein each generation should be redistributed fairly in all the social positions according to the individuals' projects and merit. In this model, justice commands that workers' children have the same opportunities as executives' children of becoming executives in turn without threatening the position discrepancy between workers and executives. Similarly, the model of opportunities implies that women are present on a par in all levels of society without transforming the ladder of professional activities and of incomes. This aspect of social justice also compels taking into account so-called ethnic and cultural "diversity" so that it is represented at all levels of social life.

The equality of opportunities radically changes the representation of society. Social classes are replaced with groups defined by the discriminations inflicted upon them by reason of their "race", their culture, their sex and their "handicaps". As these stigmata are negative, each of these actors denounces these discriminations and simultaneously asserts a demand for *recognition*, forming as many positive characteristics, cultural and social features which cement a multifarious society. Also, the representation of society changes completely when minorities are substituted for social classes. The associations, the various agencies fighting against discrimination gradually replace labor unions by demanding quotas and by initiating legal proceedings against discrimination. The modes of political representation are then understandably quite upset. The "blind" social contract gives way to more individual contracts, engaging each individual's responsibility to endeavour to emphasize his/her merit and hence maximize chances. If s/he succeeds, all the better; if s/he fails, too bad.

This model of justice may be criticized for reasons opposite to those addressed to the equality of places. First of all, the equality of opportunities does not seem to reduce social inequalities; the countries which apply this principle of social justice (the United-States and United Kingdom especially) are more inegalitarian than social-democrat and corporatist countries. The equality of opportunities admittedly does not specify which inequalities are intolerable and simply offers a survival net to the poorest. The definition of unfairness in terms of discrimination triggers a competition mechanism in victims whose interest is to "expose" their discriminations so as to benefit from specific policies. At the end of the day, the myriad of minorities supersedes the myriad of corporations. Finally, the equality of opportunities is not straightforwardly more liberal, or more favorable to autonomy than the equality of places. The conservatism of places is substituted for by rigorous merit since everyone must be fully responsible for what happens to him/her. Thus, the governments that emphasize the equality of opportunities are quite often the most conservative, in fact, the most inclined to "blame the victims" inasmuch as they failed to seize their opportunities.

Equality of places in society

Nevertheless, wanting both the equality of *places* and the equality of *opportunities* does not dispense with choosing the order of our priorities. Indeed, in *practical* terms, social policies and political programs will not be exactly the same according to whether emphasis is first set on *places* or on *opportunities*. For example, asserting that increased low wages and improved life conditions in poorer areas is one thing, outlining the crucial need to see to it that children living in these areas stand the same chances as others of becoming part of the workforce according to their merit so as to break free from their initial condition is another. I can either abolish an unfair social position or enable individuals to break free without jeopardizing said position; and even if I want to do both, I have to choose what to do *first*. In a rich society which still must establish priorities, choosing to improve the quality of the educational offer in underprivileged areas does not equate with helping the most deserving among underprivileged pupils to grant them the opportunity of joining the school and social elite. To choose a more explicit example, making sure that members of ethno-racial minorities are fairly represented in the Parliament and in the media is not the same as guaranteeing that the jobs they occupy in the building trades and civil engineering works are better paid and less hard. The argument stating that in an ideal world everything should be done at once does not stand against the imperatives of political action where what seemingly is the most important and the most decisive must inevitably be decided. We may desire the equality of places as much as the equality of opportunities, but if we want to do more than talk a lot of hot air, we cannot but choose the path which seems the fairest and the most efficient and we must grant priority to one of these two conceptions of justice.

The choice is all the more necessary since both of these models of social justice are not solely and equally indisputable theoretical working drawings. In practice, they are carried by different social movements, favoring different groups and interests. They do not mobilize and do not *build* exactly the same actors and the same interests. I do not come across and I do not act in the same manner according to whether I am fighting to improve my place in society or to increase my *chances* of escaping my position. In the first case, the actor is generally defined by his/her work, "function", "usefulness" and by his/her exploitation. In the second case, s/he is defined by his/her identity, his/her "nature" and by discriminations to which she is confronted as a woman, as a stigmatized minority, etc. Of course, both of these manners of defining oneself, of mobilizing one's efforts and of acting in pubic space are legitimate, but they cannot be merged and, again, we must choose which one should be granted priority. We need not reify the social classes on the one hand or the "minorities" on the other, to understand that a society cannot be perceived and does not act upon itself in the same manner according to whether it chooses *places* first or *opportunities* first.

If I defend the priority of the equality of places, I do not wish to deny any legitimacy to the justice of *opportunities* and of merit, but I am doing so for two essential reasons.

According to the former, the notion of equality, arguing for tighter social structure, is "good" for individuals and for their autonomy; it increases confidence and social cohesion inasmuch as actors do not engage in continuous competition, consisting in being successful as well as in exposing one's victim status in order to benefit from a specific policy. The equality of places, although always relative, creates a system of debts and of rights leading to thinking that we have more in common than distinctions and, in this sense, it strengthens solidarity. The aim of the equality of places is not the perfect community of utopias and communist nightmares, but to enhance the quality of social life and, consequently, that of personal autonomy since my freedom of action is all the greater since I am not threatened by excessive social inequalities. In so doing, it does not depart from liberal political philosophy, even if it leads to mastering and limiting the free play of economic liberalism. In short, the greatest possible equality is good "in itself" providing it does not question the individuals' autonomy and, even more so, it is desirable because it strengthens such autonomy.

The second argument in favor of the priority given to the equality of places lies in that it is undoubtedly the best manner for achieving the equality of opportunities. If the opportunities are defined as the possibility of moving around in the social structure, of going up and down the rungs of the social ladder, according to one's merit and one's value, this fluidity is obviously all the greater since the distance between places is short, meaning that those who are climbing do not face too many obstacles and those going down do not risk losing everything. Contrary to legend, there is more social mobility in France than in the United-States where the distances between the diverse social positions are greater than in France. Indeed, in its very principle, calling for the equality of opportunities does not say anything about the social inequalities between social conditions, and the latter may be so great that individuals may never overcome them, with the exception of a few heroes who might be seen as the tree of fluidity concealing the forest of immobility or, to say it quickly, propaganda heroes. In spite of the wisdom which Rawls coins the "principle of difference," which invites us to see to it that the equality of opportunities does not degrade the condition of the least privileged, one cannot fail to note that inequalities have worsened even more where *opportunities* were granted priority over *places*.

* * *

Defending the priority of the equality of places must not be confused with fighting for keeping the Welfare State as it is. It does not induce to ignore the serious criticisms addressed by all *outsiders*, by all those who cannot benefit from it. The struggle for the equality of places hence requires considering far-reaching reforms of the Welfare State and of public services. It also involves breaking from a few traditional political left-wing clienteles who tend to maximize the interests of such systems, it also requires reviewing the system of social transfers so as to know, really, who pays and who gains. In all cases, it implies somehow tearing away the "veil of ignorance", that deep-rooted opacity.

2 Stability and Increasing Fluidity in the Contemporary Japanese Social Stratification System*

Yoshimichi Sato

The coexistence of stability and increasing fluidity in the social stratification system

We argue that stability and increasing fluidity coexist in the contemporary Japanese social stratification system. It is often argued that the weakening of Japanese employment practice has made the labor market more flexible. While there is evidence to support this argument, it misses an important factor in the labor market, namely social stratification. We predict that some parts of the labor market have become more fluid, while other parts have remained stable. This prediction is derived from our assumption that protective institutions in the labor market have their own inertia (Sato and Arita 2008). Inertia of a local institution refers to how irresponsive it is to global factors such as globalization and neoliberal policies. A local institution has small inertia if it quickly responds to global factors, while it has large inertia if it responds slowly or not at all to them.

We argue that protective institutions in the internal labor market have larger inertia than those in the external labor market. This is because employers in the internal labor market still need, or at least believe they need, "core employees" to work for them until retirement.[1] Additionally, labor unions in the internal labor market are eager to maintain the job security of their members, even though their influence has been declining. In contrast, employers in the external labor market find it more difficult than before to provide their employees with job security, and labor unions are either politically weak or do not exist in the external labor market.

It is therefore predicted that this differential inertia, which is created by class strategies (Ishida and Slater 2010) of various social classes in the labor market, produces the coexistence of stability in the internal labor market and increasing fluidity in the external labor market. Furthermore, people in higher strata dominate in the internal labor market, while people in lower strata are pushed to the external labor market. Thus this prediction leads to another prediction, namely that the working and living conditions of people in lower strata have been deteriorating because of increasing fluidity in the external labor market.

In this paper we present evidence that supports these theoretical predictions. The evidence comes from findings of the 2005 Social Stratification and Social Mobility Survey Project (SSM) (Principal Investigator: Sato Yoshimichi). This project studies social stratification, social mobility, and inequality using data sets obtained by nationwide surveys conducted every decade since 1955. In the 2005 SSM Project we hypothesized that stability and fluidity coexist in the labor market, based on theories of the dual labor market in Japan (Odaka 1984; Kalleberg and Lincoln 1988; Nomura 1994). What we found by analyzing the data sets, however, is not fluidity but increasing fluidity and, therefore, the coexistence of stability and increasing fluidity. Theories of the dual labor market, which focus on differences between small and mid-size firms and large firms, seem to have implicitly assumed that most workers have regular jobs. However, the sharp increase in the number of non-regular workers as well as the emergence of new types of non-regular workers such as temporary employees has led to increasing fluidity. Thus we need to differentiate between the regular and non-regular employment sectors to properly analyze the coexistence of stability and increasing fluidity in the dual labor market (Imai and Sato, forthcoming).

From this perspective, in the following sections we will discuss education and inequality, increasing fluidity and disparity among young workers, job changes, and income inequality,[2] in order to fully understand the current situation of inequality and social stratification in contemporary Japan.

Education and inequality

Two topics will be discussed in this section: transition from school to work and entry into regular/non-regular employment. The implicit contract is an informal relationship between local schools and firms that facilitates the smooth transition from school to work (Kariya 1991). Teachers exchange information with company recruiters on high school students and job openings. Teachers then recommend particular students for jobs in particular firms with an implicit guarantee for the students, and the firms hire the recommended students trusting the teachers' evaluation of them. The implicit contract is supported by trusting relationships between teachers and recruiters and the efficient exchange of information about students and jobs. It is a key to the low unemployment rates of young people in Japan compared to their counterparts in other advanced societies.

Honda (2005), however, argues that the implicit contract is weakening. This argument seems reasonable, because firms can no longer maintain the contract due to their exposure to increasing fluidity in the labor market, thus explaining why many high school students find it difficult to get a regular job upon graduation. Using SSM data sets, Brinton (2008) analyzed the processes by which young people enter their first jobs. She compared three graduation cohorts: the older cohort (graduating from school before 1978), the bubble-economy cohort (graduating from school between 1978 and 1991), and the post-bubble-economy cohort (graduating from school between 1992 and 2005). The proportion of those who got a job by implicit contract was 40.4 percent in the pre-bubble-economy cohort, 41.91 percent in the bubble-economy cohort, and 37.59 percent in the post-bubble-economy cohort. Although the proportion for the post-bubble-economy cohort is smaller, the difference to the other cohorts is not statistically significant. This means that the implicit contract has not necessarily been weakening.

By using entry to regular employment as the dependent variable in logistic regression analysis, Brinton (2008) also shows that those who got a job through implicit contract are more likely to get a job within a month of graduation and to get a regular job than those who directly apply for work through job advertisements. This result shows that an implicit contract is still a powerful tool with which to get a regular job upon graduation. Furthermore, it also suggests that young people who are unable to use the implicit contract find it more difficult than before to obtain a regular job in the contemporary labor market. This is because non-regular employment accounts for an increasing share of the market.

Entry to regular employment is also affected by educational stratification. Better-educated people are more likely to enter regular employment (Brinton 2008). Using the 2005 SSM data set, Hirata (2008) shows that less-educated people are more likely to enter non-regular employment and have been more exposed to the negative impacts of the recession since 1992. Many specialists in the study of young part-time workers (*freeters* in Japanese), such as Kosugi

(2002; 2003), point out that less-educated people are more likely to become freeters, a finding that supports the conclusions of Brinton and Hirata.

These findings show that stability and increasing fluidity coexist in contemporary Japanese educational stratification. On the one hand, well-educated people and those who are able to use an implicit contract have an advantage in getting a regular job. On the other hand, those who are unable to use an implicit contract tend to enter non-regular employment. In addition, as will be shown, once a person enters non-regular employment, he/she tends to stay in that sector. Thus we argue that the upper educational strata enjoy stability, while the lower educational strata are involved in the turmoil of the fluid labor market.

Increasing fluidity and disparity among youth

Young people are the ones who are most deeply affected by the increasing fluidity of the labor market in Japan. Mass media often focuses on the difficulties faced by young workers, who are often characterized as freeters, NEETs, and working poor.[3] This section examines the situation of young workers from the viewpoint of social stratification.

Long-term employment is still prevalent in large firms and the public sector. Using event history analysis, Nakazawa (2008) analyzed the effect of stratification variables on the duration of a young person's first job. Figure 2.1 displays the coefficient of firm size by gender after controlling for other variables. The coefficient for the mid-size firm is 0 because this is the reference category. Thus a positive (negative) coefficient for another category means a longer (shorter) duration in the first job compared to mid-size firms. Because the coefficients for large firms and the public sector are positive in the case of male workers, men who get their first job at large firms or in the public sector tend to hold the job longer than their counterparts in small and mid-size firms. The figure also clearly shows the gender difference in the duration of a young person's first job. Coefficients for female workers at large firms and the public sector are not as large as those of their male counterparts.

Those who enter the public sector for their first job recently also tend to stay there for longer (Nakazawa 2008). Nakazawa's comparison of the duration of first job between entry cohorts shows that those who entered the sector after 1992 had a stronger tendency

Figure 2.1: The effect of company size on duration of first job

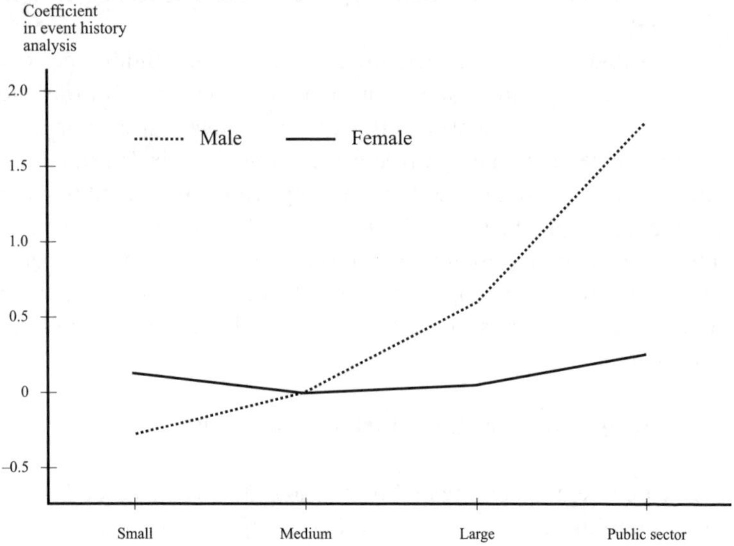

[Figure: Line graph. Y-axis: "Coefficient in event history analysis", ranging from -0.5 to 2.0. X-axis categories: Small, Medium, Large, Public sector. Two lines: Male (dotted) rising from about -0.25 at Small to about 1.8 at Public sector; Female (solid) roughly flat near 0, slightly rising to about 0.25 at Public sector.]

Source: Drawn by the author based on Nakazawa (2008: 128, Table 5)

to stay than cohorts entering the sector before 1992. This may indicate that people in the more recent entry cohort stayed in their first public sector job because it would be difficult for them to get a better job elsewhere.

These results imply that the long-term employment practice is still prevalent in the core of the labor market, but it is more difficult for young people to obtain regular employment upon graduation. Thus a disparity emerges between those who enjoy high job security and those who only manage to enter unstable jobs. Because well-educated people are more likely to get a job at large firms and in the public sector, Nakazawa's findings suggest increasing inequality of job security between educational strata.

Nakazawa analyzed the core of the dual labor market in Japan. Graduates who first obtain only non-regular jobs find it difficult to move into regular employment. Sato Kaoru (2008) confirmed this by analyzing the effect of entering non-regular jobs on occupational career trajectories. Her analysis shows that if a person's first job is non-regular, there is an increased possibility that the person's current job is also non-regular. This is the case both for men and women.

Figure 2.2: Proportions of female regular/non-regular workers by education and birth cohort

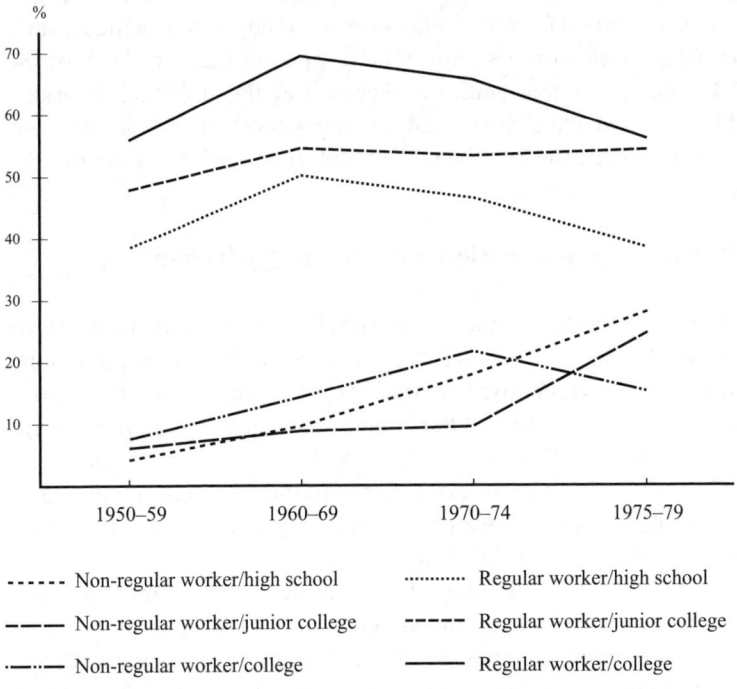

- - - - - Non-regular worker/high school   ············ Regular worker/high school
——— Non-regular worker/junior college   - - - - Regular worker/junior college
·—··— Non-regular worker/college   ——— Regular worker/college

Source: Drawn by the author based on Iwai (2008: 94, Table 2)

Increasing fluidity is also occurring in the early life courses of Japanese women. Iwai (2008) shows that the life course of women has become more diversified. He calculated the proportion of female regular and non-regular workers at the age of 25 by birth cohort and education. Figure 2.2 demonstrates that the proportion of women with regular jobs declined between the 1960–1969 birth cohort and the 1975–1979 birth cohort, with the exception of junior college graduates. The figure also shows that, in the case of the youngest cohort, the proportions of non-regular workers for high school and junior college graduates increase, while for college graduates it decreases. These results reflect the increasing difficulty of getting a regular job for young Japanese women regardless of education, as well as the increased risks associated with entering non-regular employment for young less-educated women.

These findings suggest that the increase in the share of non-regular workers and the increasing fluidity of employment are not ubiquitous in the youth labor market. Well-educated workers tend to be still under the protection of the long-term employment practice, while less-educated workers tend to be trapped in the periphery of the labor market as non-regular workers during the prolonged recession. Therefore we should not study young workers as a homogeneous group. Rather, the coexistence of stability and increasing fluidity should be emphasized.

Heterogeneous situations surrounding job changers

Increasing fluidity in the labor market naturally leads to the study of job changes. Nobody has the same probability of changing jobs; some people with particular stratification characteristics may have a higher probability than other people. Thus in this section we focus on job changes from the viewpoint of social stratification. From this perspective we explore changes in the long-term employment practice over time, as well as the meaning of occupational licenses and certificates in the labor market.

Although the weakening of the long-term employment practice has led to an increase in the number and frequency of job changes, there is evidence to suggest that this weakening has not occurred ubiquitously across social strata. There are important differences in stratification characteristics between those who stay in their jobs and those who change. To analyze the effect of firm size and occupation on long term-employment practice, Inada (2008) calculated the proportion of workers in the long-term employment practice among white-collar workers at large firms, white-collar workers at small and mid-size firms, blue-collar workers at large firms, and blue-collar workers at small and mid-size firms by entry cohort. The calculation reveals that the percentage of workers in the long-term employment practice declined for all groups between the 1976–1985 entry cohort (i.e., the youngest cohort) and the 1966–1975 entry cohort, suggesting that the long-term employment practice has recently weakened. What is more important, however, is that this decline is steeper for workers at small and mid-size firms than for those at large firms. Inada's calculation shows that the weakening of the long-term employment practice has not occurred ubiquitously in the labor market. In other words, the gap between small/mid-size and large firms has become wider in terms of the long-term employment practice.

Figure 2.3: Proportion of job changes resulting in income reduction across educational strata and over time

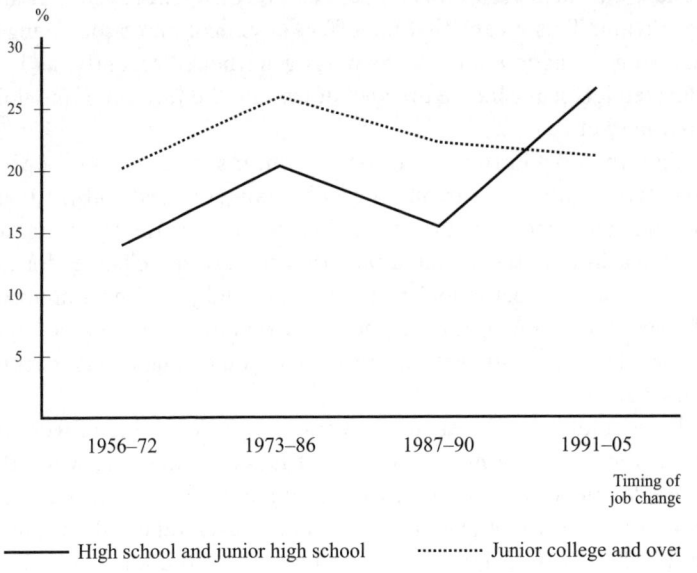

Source: Drawn by the author based on Hayashi (2008: 64, Table 2)

Hirata's (2008) event history analysis reveals that women are more likely than men to leave their first job, and non-regular workers are more likely than regular workers to leave their job. Workers at larger firms and in the public sector in particular are less likely to leave their job. These findings complement those of Nakazawa (2008) discussed above.

If a person changes jobs to improve his or her working conditions, there is no problem. But Yoshida (2008a) shows that changing jobs at an early stage of career development generally results in a reduction of income. He also shows that if a person changes jobs within three years of getting the first job, he or she mitigates to a degree the negative effect on their income so long as they do not leave the job afterward. However, according to Yoshida, it is difficult to hold on to the second job.

Hayashi (2008) calculated the proportion of job changes that resulted in income reduction across educational strata. Figure 2.3 shows how this proportion changed over time. The proportion of job changes resulting in income reduction was higher for the well-educated group until 1987–1990, although the difference between the two groups was not statistically significant. However, in 1991–2005 the proportion for the less-educated group was higher, and the difference is statistically significant. This means that the effect of education on job changes resulting in income reductions has strengthened recently, as less-educated job changers are dragged down into the turmoil of the fluid labor market.

The above-mentioned findings demonstrate the worsening objective conditions surrounding job changers. And, subjectively, job changers recognize the worsening situation in the labor market. Kanbayashi (2008) calculated the proportion of job changes for the reason "I found a better job" by birth cohort and year. The proportion of men who changed jobs in their 20s was lower for the younger cohort. This suggests that the situation of job changers has recently worsened.

Even voluntary job changes can result in a worsening of working conditions. According to theories of labor economics, when the unemployment rate is high, involuntary job changes such as layoffs increase while voluntary job changes decrease. Takenoshita (2008) shows that the unemployment rate increased voluntary as well as involuntary job changes during 1986–2005, but did not affect either in 1953–1985. He attributes this to the following mechanism: Normally, if a worker found a job he (or she) preferred, he would not easily change it, even if his current work-place is not very good. However, mismatch between workers and jobs occurred more frequently among young workers during the 1990s, a period of prolonged recession. Because of this mismatch, even slight dissatisfaction with workplace conditions could drive workers to change jobs.

Under these fluid labor market conditions workers need "weapons" to protect themselves. Job certificates and licenses are examples of such weapons. Agata (2008) examined whether workers use certificates and licenses that are relevant to their occupation. His logistic regression analysis with use/non-use as the dependent variable shows that less-educated workers use their certificates and licenses more effectively. Based on this result, he argues that "while well-educated people are likely to have opportunities for better jobs without certificates and licenses, less-educated people tend to develop their careers by getting relevant certificates and licenses because they cannot rely on their school diplomas" (Agata 2008: 98). In other words, degrees of higher education are still effective even in the fluid labor market, providing further evidence of the stability in the core of the labor market.

These findings demonstrate the coexistence of stability and increasing fluidity in the circumstances surrounding job changes. As Inada (2008) points out, the long-term employment practice has not weakened in large firms as rapidly as in small and mid-size firms. In the external labor market, however, job changes with income reductions occur more frequently, and the reasons for job changes become worse. Job changers of this kind tend to be workers at small and mid-size firms and non-regular workers, many of whom try to improve their standing in the harsh labor market by getting certificates and licenses.

Widening income disparity and immobility

Analysis of income using the SSM data set shows a mild increase in inequality of household income from 1995 to 2005 (Aizawa and Miwa 2008; Kanomata 2008). Analysis of income inequality between occupations shows that the gap of income between professionals and other occupations has widened (Sato 2008; Nagamatsu 2008). Nagamatsu explains this by two mechanisms. First, the demand for highly skilled labor has increased, while that for low-skilled labor has decreased. This mechanism is called the skill-biased technological change hypothesis. Second, the wage of low-skilled labor has been suppressed due to harsh competition between firms.

While income inequality reveals inequality of outcome, inequality of income transmission over generations captures inequality of opportunity to earn an income. Using the 1995 and 2005 SSM data sets and by estimating the father's income, Yoshida (2008b) created an intergenerational mobility (transmission) table of income. He divided income distribution by quartiles and created the transmission table by year and birth cohort. His analysis reveals a strong association between the father's and the child's income for the lowest and the highest strata. In addition, in the case of respondents aged 45–54 who have almost accomplished their occupational attainment, the association became stronger at the lowest as well as the highest stratum, and the rate of change towards stronger association is steeper for the highest stratum than that for the lowest stratum.

The above-mentioned analyses of income in this section show increasing inequality and immobility. The income of professionals has increased relative to that of other occupations; intergenerational transmission of income is fixed at the highest and the lowest strata; and the transmission has become more immobile at the highest strata in particular.

Heterogeneous changes in the stratification structure

We have examined findings from the 2005 SSM Project focusing on education and inequality, increasing fluidity and disparity among young workers, job changes, and income inequality. Based on these findings, we could argue that some parts of the social stratification system are still under protective institutions, while other parts of it are showing signs of increasing fluidity. We argue that strata in the core of the labor market are stable, while the level of fluidity is increasing in the periphery, based on such phenomena as the strength of the implicit contract, the widening gap of the long-term employment practice between small/mid-size and large firms, the strong association between educational attainment and employment status (regular and non-regular), heterogeneous situations surrounding job changers, the meaning of certificates and licenses, the relative increase in the income of professionals, and increasing immobility of intergenerational income transmission. Nakazawa, who analyzed the employment situation of youth, describes the situation as follows:

> [T]he increase in non-regular workers in their first and second job is noticeable. That is, non-regular workers tend to leave a job or to change jobs because their job security is low in general. This leads to increasing fluidity of the labor market. On the other hand, there is no tendency that the duration of employment of regular workers has become shorter recently. (Nakazawa 2008: 128)

That is, there is no change in the core of the labor market, but the periphery is increasingly fluid. Thus the level of fluidity seems to be increasing as a whole.

An important research question arises: Why has the level of fluidity been increasing in the periphery of the labor market? As mentioned above, Nagamatsu (2008) points out that income disparity between occupational strata is caused by skill-biased technological change and the suppression of the income of low-skilled workers. This explanation focuses on changes in the relationship between demand and supply in the labor market.

However, another explanation addressing segmentation in the labor market exists. According to the rent hypothesis proposed by Grusky Weeden and Di Carlo (2008), the recent rapid increase in income gap is attributable to the creation of rent at high strata and the collapse of rent at low strata. They define rent as a gap between actual wage and the wage that would be earned if there were no entry barrier. For example, if only union members may work in a particular job, non-union members who are willing to work at a lower wage than that of union members cannot get the job. Thus union members earn the difference between the two wages as a rent. Professionals such as lawyers and medical doctors who need an official certificate to get a job also earn rent. Grusky et al. argue that rents at lower strata have been deteriorating due to such factors as the weakening of labor unions, while rents at higher strata have been created by such social closure as the increase in the number of occupations that require official certificates.

Nagamatsu (2008) and Grusky et al.'s (2008) arguments are about income, but they can be applied to job security and benefit packages as well. Applying them to the labor market in Japan would show that its duality, which is a distinctive feature of it, has been reinforced; that is, higher strata are still protected in the core of the labor market due to increasing demand for them and the creation of rents, while lower strata are trapped in the increasing fluidity of the market periphery due to the deterioration of rents. This complements the theoretical argument, outlined in the first section, that protective institutions in the internal labor market have larger inertia than those in the external labor market. Protective institutions in Japan have produced rents, and their inertia is large. Thus workers in the internal (core) labor market still enjoy rents, while those in the periphery suffer a deterioration of rents, contributing to an increase in the number of non-regular workers.

The functional theory of social stratification once argued that social stratification exists because it has positive functions in society (Davis and Moore 1945; Parsons 1940). In addition, Hara and Seiyama (2005) point out that social stratification has public values that link individuals' motivation to the order of social stratification. However, the emerging characteristic of social stratification in contemporary Japan—the coexistence of stability and increasing fluidity—casts doubt on such social functions and public values. Rather, focusing on class strategies (Ishida and Slater 2010) such as the creation of rents in the labor market would lead to a better understanding and explanation of changes in Japan's social stratification system.[4]

3 The Paradoxa of Exclusion: Crossed Considerations on the Contemporary Forms of Broken Social Links

Serge Paugam

The notion of social exclusion is part of the sociological language. Several research programmes in France and in Europe have been dedicated to it (Paugam, 1996). But it also corresponds to a social issue for which numerous actions and policies are conducted. It is therefore sometimes difficult to dissociate the scientific usage from the social usage of this notion, which may occasionally generate misunderstandings. Its meaning has also evolved significantly since its emergence in France in the mid-1960s, in a period of economic prosperity, which is interesting in itself from a sociological perspective, but which does not facilitate the establishment of a stable and homogeneous definition. Exclusion could not occupy, in the 1970s, a prominent position in the political debate since the latter fed almost exclusively on the issue of inequalities and their reproduction. Today, the debate does not rest mainly on unequal society any longer, not so much because inequalities would have disappeared, but because they do not suffice any longer, for their own part, to explain phenomena such as identity break-up and crisis which characterize the process of exclusion.

The suburb issue, for instance cannot be explained by the forms of spatial segregation and inequalities in terms of housing alone. It also encompasses a process wherein social relations are deteriorating within underprivileged residential areas and the increasing difficulties of the population in coping with feelings of loneliness, boredom, emptiness, etc. The notion of exclusion successfully encompasses, at least implicitly, a crisis of social links. While still referring to the thematic of inequalities, the notion of exclusion goes beyond it by conferring a new meaning, one no longer based essentially on conflicting interests between social groups and the struggle for social recognition, but rather on the weakness, even the absence of organized claims and movements likely to strengthen identity cohesion among underprivileged populations.

This evolution in the perception of the phenomena is also visible at the level of the European Union. From a static definition of poverty based on a monetary approach, the definition is now dynamic and multidimensional. For certain experts of Eurostat and communautary programmes on underprivileged populations, the notion of exclusion offered, at the beginning of the 1990s, an alternative to both the methodological and conceptual dead ends to which the conventional work on measuring poverty had led.

The social debate still nurtures numerous preconceived ideas that the researchers in social sciences endeavour to put into question while looking for the fundamental paradigms to which the notion of exclusion refers. These preconceived ideas are fuelled by the media. Journalists are often on the look-out for sensationalism and do not always pay great heed to the representativity of the examples they quote and to the (often caricatural) pictures of reality that they produce. Regarding socially and politically sensitive issues as exclusion, researchers generally admit that there is no such thing as an absolute definition. These are relative notions which may vary according to time and place. It is unreasonable to claim that a fair, objective scientific definition (one distinct from the social debate) can be found without falling into the trap of specific population categorizations when it goes without saying that the boundaries which differentiate them from other social groups are never clear and viable once and for all. To want to define "the excluded" according to precise (supposedly scientific) criteria leads in fact to reify new social categories, or categories similar to those built socially, thereby letting on that a science of poverty or of exclusion may exist independently from the specific cultural context of each society. Since we have to admit that a scientific poverty or exclusion threshold is impossible to define, any theoretical approach to these fuzzy notions is bound to set in stone and to validate categorizations which, in reality, are always arbitrary and unavoidably fluctuating.

We shall assume here that exclusion is a cumulative breaking process of social links. It is therefore necessary to go back to the sources of social links to understand the mechanisms thereof, all the more so since research in the field is going from strength to strength.

The elementary and interlaced forms of social links

It is important to take into account the anthropological interlacing of social links and the multiple ways in which individuals are attached to society. The social link would then be the product of this interlaced multiplicity of links and what is called the "crisis of social links" would correspond to questioning, at least partially, said interlacing. Whereas in mechanical solidarity societies (Durkheim 2007[/1893]), belonging to the group grants individuals protection against external threats and immediate recognition of their social status, in organic solidarity societies, with their more generalized protection systems, recognition becomes an autonomous stake for the individuals.

Every type of social link can be defined from both dimensions of protection and recognition. The links are multiple and of different nature, but they all provide individuals with both the *protection* and the *recognition* necessary for their social existence (Paugam 2008). Protection encompasses all the supports which the individual can mobilize to cope with life contingencies (family, communautary, professional, social resources, etc), recognition refers to the social interaction which stimulates the individual by supplying the proof of his existence and his valorization in other people's eyes. The expression "to count on" is a fair summary of what the individual may expect from his or her relationship with others and with institutions in terms of protection, while the expression "to count for" expresses the expectation (which is just as vital) for recognition. The affective investment in a "we" is all the stronger since said "we" corresponds to the entity (which may be as real as abstract) whereon and for which the person knows s/he may count. It is in this sense that the "we" is constitutive of the "I". The links which secure protection and recognition to the individual hence take on an affective dimension that reinforces human interdependencies.

Continuing this reflection, four major types of social links may be differentiated: the *filiation link*, the *elective participation link*, the *organic participation link* and the *citizenship link* (see Table 3.1).

The *filiation link* takes on two different forms. The form which first of all comes to mind refers to consanguinity, that is to say the so-called "natural" filiation which is founded on the evidence of sexual relationships between the father and the mother and on the recognition of a biological parenthood between the child and his/her genitors. The initial observation is that every individual is born in a family and theoretically meets at birth both his/her father and mother, as well as an extended family to which s/he belongs without having chosen it. Still, the adoptive filiation recognized by the Civil Law and which ought to be distinguished from the family placement, should not be left aside. The adoptive filiation is somehow a social filiation. More generally speaking, let us bear in mind that the filiation link, in its biological or adoptive dimension, constitutes the absolute foundation of social belonging. Let us also note that by virtue of the principle of consanguinity, the children are entitled to inherit from their parents, but on grounds of nutritional obligation, said parents are compelled to look after said children. Beyond the legal issues regarding the definition of the filiation link, sociologists, but also psychologists, social psychologists and psychoanalysts, insist on the socialising and identity function of this link. It contributes to the balance of the individual as of his/her birth since it secures protection, physical care (and recognition) as well as affective safety to him/her.

The *elective participation link* refers to the extra-family socialization during which the individual comes in contact with other individuals whom s/he comes to know in the context of various groups and institutions. The places for this socialization are numerous: neighbourhoods, gangs, groups of friends, local communities as well as religious, sportive, cultural institutions, etc. In the course of his social trainings, the individual is constrained by the necessity of integrations, but at the same time autonomous inasmuch as he may himself build up his network of memberships from which he may assert his personality under the others' gaze. This link should not be confused with a thesis according to which social links would be today founded on a multiplicity of memberships of elective nature or on a positive disaffiliation process (Singly 2003). It would be appropriate indeed to distinguish the elective participation link from the other social link by highlighting its specificity, namely its elective character which leaves individuals truly free to establish interpersonal relationships to suit their desires, their aspirations and their emotional valences. This link covers several forms of non-constrained attachment. The formation of the couple may be considered as one of them. The individual integrates into another family network than his own. He widens his circle of membership. Whereas in the *filiation link*, the individual has no freedom of choice, he enjoys a certain autonomy with the *elective participation link*. Said autonomy however is restricted by a series of social determinations. The conjugal relationship besides is akin to a game of mirrors. In addition to the protection function it provides to husband and wife (wherein they may rely upon one another), the recognition function may be addressed in four ways: the way the husband looks upon his wife, the way the wife looks upon her husband and finally the way each of them judges the other's look. It is thus a game when every partner can be valorized by regularly demonstrating how much the other's presence is crucial. Unlike family and couple, friendship is little institutionalized. It may be mentioned and encouraged publicly when associated for instance with the notion of fraternity, but it is not governed by strict regulation. It is socially recognized and valorized. It fits in perfectly with the definition of the elective participation link. It is perceived as disinterested and as detached from the social contingencies which characterize the other forms of sociability.

The *organic participation link* differentiates from the previous one in that it is characterized by learning and exercising a set function in the organization of work. According to Durkheim, the social link in modern societies (the organic solidarity) rests first of all, as seen above, on the complementarity of functions, which confers to all individuals, however different they may be from one another, a social position liable to provide both the elementary protection and the feeling of being useful. This link is woven into the context of the school and grows into the world of work. If this type of link becomes meaningful in the light of the productive logic of industrial society, it should not be conceived as exclusively dependent on the economic sphere. As highlighted by Elias (1991), in the societies characterized by a high interdependent level of functions, economy is not an autonomous sphere. It cannot evolve without a parallel evolution of the political and State organization. The establishment of a compulsory social insurance system founded on employment activity has contributed to modify the very meaning of professional integration. To analyse the organic participation link, not only the relation to work in accordance with Durkheim's analysis, but also the relation to employment, which is subjected to the protective logic of the social State, should be taken into consideration. In other words, professional integration does not solely mean self-fulfilment at work, but also being covered, beyond the world of work, by the elementary protection framework built on social struggles in the context of a welfare policy. The expression "to have a job" means for the wage-earners the possibility of self-fulfilment in a productive activity and, at the same time, secured guarantees so as to cope with the future. The ideal type of professional integration can hence be defined as the double insurance of material and symbolic recognition of work and of the social protection system which comes with the job.

Finally, the *citizenship link* is based on the principle of belonging to a nation. As a matter of principle, the nation grants rights and duties to its members and bestows full citizenship upon them. In democratic societies, citizens are equal by right, which means not so much that economic and social inequalities disappear, but that efforts have been made in the nation so that all the citizens are treated on a par and form together a corpus with common identity and values. The civil rights which protect the individual in the exercise of his/her fundamental freedom, especially against supposedly illegitimate trespassing by the State, as well as the political rights which grant him/her participation in public life are commonly differentiated from the social rights which secure him/her a certain protection to cope with life contingencies. This extension process of the individual fundamental rights corresponds to the consecration of the universal principle of equality and of the role devolved to the citizen-individual who is supposed to belong "by operation of law", beyond the specificity of his/her social status, to the political community. The citizenship link is also founded on the recognition of the citizen's sovereignty. Article 6 of the Universal Declaration of Human Rights reads: "The law is the expression of the general will. All citizens have the right to contribute personally, or through their representatives, to its formation." It also takes its rise in the protective logic of democratic equality. The citizen-individual must have "the required material means to remain that independent and self-sufficient being who underpins political legitimacy. The organization of education, of work protection, of assistance to the people in distress is justified in that citizens must have the ability to be autonomous" (Schnapper 2000: 32). There again, the citizenship link encompasses bases for both the protection and recognition that we have already identified in the three previous types of links. The citizenship link is based on a demanding conception of the individual's rights and duties.

These four types of links are complementary and interlaced. They form the social fabric around the individual. When someone makes claims of his/her identity, he may refer to his nationality (*citizenship link*), occupation (*organic participation link*), groups of membership (*elective participation link*), or family origins (*filiation link*). In every society, these four types of links form the social web which pre-exists individuals and which they may rely on to weave their memberships to the social corpus through the socialization process. If the intensity of these social links varies from one individual to the other according to the particular conditions of its socialization, it also depends on the relative prominence ascribed by the societies. The role played for example by family solidarities and collective expectations varies from one society to the other. The forms of sociability derived from the elective participation link or the organic participation link are multifarious, depending to a vast extent on lifestyle. The prominence ascribed to the principle of citizenship as the basis for protection and for recognition is not the same in all countries.

But more generally speaking, when universal protection is at least partially questioned, individuals look for complementary forms of protection in their private sphere, with the effect of increasing inequalities. Facing the risk of losing both self-respect and self-esteem in an open and liberated society, many may be strongly tempted to go back to more communautary modes of social organization and withdraw into traditional identity forms. This is also why the social link cannot be analysed without referring to the plurality of the links binding the individual to the groups and to society as a whole. In other words, the global transformation of societies is characterized not only by a transformation of social links, but also by a gradual redefinition of the relationship between the different types of social links.

Fragility and cumulative break-up of social links

The fragility of social links essentially lies in the significant risk of their breaking. To study social links hence implies not only analyzing the multiplicity and intensity of social links, but also their fragility, in the sense of their possible breaking. The fragility of social links is due to both of their sources: protection and recognition.

Still, protection and recognition are today fragilized. The generalized protection system set up during the 20th century has clearly lost ground and numerous fringes of the population are increasingly precarious or threatened with becoming so. The recognition provided by stable attachment to restricted social groups (and the formal participation constraints deriving therefrom) today involves greater autonomy, even emancipation, of the individual relative to his/her traditional attachments, which confers him/her greater margin of interpretation of the collective standards, but simultaneously fragilizes his/her identity since the latter is subjected to other people's looks and consequently to denial or contempt threats. The precarized individual is somehow bound, at least temporarily, to experience social suffering.

Social insecurity and increased sensitivity to the forms of contempt run through the whole society. They fuel the feeling that the social link is falling apart. The sociologist must be able to study society as an entity with its own life. If society exerts a mental constraint on the

Table 3.1: Definition of the different types of link according to the forms of protection and of recognition

	Forms of protection	Forms of recognition
Filiation link (between parents and children)	Counting on intergenerational solidarity Close protection	Counting for one's parents and one's children Affective recognition
Elective participation link (between partners, friends, selected acquaintances...)	Counting on the solidarity of elective acquaintances Close protection	Counting for elective acquaintances Affective recognition or by similarity
Organic participation link (between actors of the occupational life)	Stable job Contractualized protection	Recognition through work and consequent social esteem
Citizenship link (between members of the same political community)	Legal protection (civil, political and social rights) as per the principle of equality	Recognition of the sovereign individual

individuals, these currents may be assumed to reach into individual consciences as well.

It is in this sense that Durkheim (2007[/1897]: 229) speaks of the distress in society which necessarily turns into individuals' distress. According to him, the crisis of the social link results from the relaxation of the social link, which may cause more numerous break-ups. The types of break-ups are associated with the types of social links (see Table 3.2). The purpose here is not to pass judgment on the break-up properly speaking. A broken link may be a trying experience with far-reaching consequences for the individual, but it may also turn out to be a relief or a kind of liberation.

The filiation link may be broken at an early stage. A mother who does not feel able to look after her child or to see to its education, may decide to abandon him/her when giving birth anonymously. Parents may lose their parental authority and their children may be taken away from them by judicial decision, and placed in specialized educational institutions or foster families. Placement does not equate to total break-up, but it causes to a variable extent the parents to be disqualified as such and children may then find it harder to build a positive attachment to them. Certain children, once placed in such families or institutions, sometimes refuse to see their parents. The filiation link may also be broken after the parents' death. All these situations refer to de facto situations which make any relationships between parents and children either impossible

Table 3.2: Broken social links

	Protection deficit	**Recognition denial**
Filiation link	Impossibility to count on one's parents or one's children in case of difficulty	Abandonment, bad treatments, durable disagreement, rejection
		Feeling of not counting for one's parents or one's children
Elective participation link	Relational insulation	Rejection by the group of peers
		Treason, abandonment
Organic participation link	Occasional link with the labour market	Social humiliation
		Negative identity
	Long-term unemployment	Feeling of being useless
	Entering a supported career	
Citizenship link	Distance from administrative circuits	Legal discrimination
		Non recognition of the civil, political and social rights
	Legal uncertainty	
	Vulnerability to institutions	Political apathy
	Absence of identity papers	
	Forced exile	

or episodic, possibly improbable. In other cases, the break-up is not formal, in particular when the child is still living in his parents' home, but experiences bad treatment, regular vexation and rejection. It is then a parental recognition denial with generally far-reaching and durable psychological consequences for the child. The filiation link may also be broken at an adult age. It may result from an unhappy event which causes reciprocal misunderstanding or discord. Filiation may not be broken automatically, but the link is no longer fuelled. The parents and the children then withdraw into themselves and do not expect any further protection or recognition from the relationship.

The elective participation link may be broken in several ways since this type of link covers various relationships. In modern societies, love relationships and friendships may be broken all the easier since they are generally not governed by any formal social constraints. Since everyone is free to fuel this type of relationship, everyone may also step aside freely. But it does not mean that the break-up does not cause any distress. Conjugal break-up may cause traumas and rekindle older affective wounds. It also translates in modified "I/we" and is passed on the whole relational network of the person in question regardless whether at the origin of the decision to break up. When studying the trajectory of people who have experienced a series of break-ups, divorce or couple separation often appear as a triggering factor. I recall a young man thus summing up the situation he had just gone through: "my girl left me and I went down the drain". Although this is quite a lapidary formula, it nevertheless expresses the essential character of the affective link in building identity and achieving psychological balance. Friendly relationships are also fragile. They are generally renewed during the life cycle in relation to geographic mobility. Youth friendships are not obligatorily formally broken up, but the relationships fuelling them often whither until they fade away. When lifestyles and habits diverge, it is also difficult to preserve such relationships in the long run. The result may be relational insulation, experienced as the impossibility of relying on one's next of kin or on one's former next of kin in case of difficulty. In some cases, breaking-up is experienced as recognition of denial in the form of treason or rejection. The same process may occur among peers, in a club or an association, when one of the members is banned therefrom or decides on his own, after vexations or contempt, to leave the group.

The first break-up of the organic participation link is due to unemployment, that is to say forced cessation of occupational activity, which when enduring, translates into lower standards of living. The research on experienced unemployment (Schnapper 1981; Gallie and Paugam 2000), poverty and forced appeals to assistance have enabled us to check the risk for the people affected of either being or feeling socially disqualified (Paugam 1991). In reality, precarious situations comparable to unemployment may be found in the world of work, in the forms of identity crises and weakened social links. For poor people, having to solicit social action services to obtain something to live on often alters their prior identity and impregnates all of their relationships with others. They then have the feeling of being a burden on the collective, with depreciated social status. Is the precarious wage-earner (Paugam 2000) in a comparable situation? S/he may not have to solicit assistance services systematically (although the latter increasingly welcome people with a job) but s/he belongs to a socially depreciated category. The sociological investigation shows that numerous wage-earners often have the feeling that they are kept in a demeaning condition without the slightest chance of improving their life circumstances. What they lack is dignity, i.e. honour and consideration. Their honour is flouted when they cannot fulfil themselves in their work and act in accordance with their own moral representations. They are also considered to be so lowly at work that they may feel socially downgraded, when they do not count for others or do not count any longer. For the wage-earners close to *uncertain integration* (or insecure integration which combines high-quality and low security jobs), the impossible stabilization of their occupational situation equates to the absence of any future. For the wage-earners close to *laborious integration* (or constrained integration: poor-quality and high-security job), distress at work is often the expression of low consideration for what they are and what they provide to the company. Finally, for the wage-earners close to *disqualifying integration* (low quality and insecure job), the cumulation of substanceless work and uncertain future is source of despair and humiliation. Wage-earners' social disqualification hence starts as soon as they are kept, against their own volition, in a situation which deprives them in all or in part of the dignity generally granted to those whose efforts contribute to the productive activity necessary to the welfare of the collectivity: a means of self-expression, a decent income, a recognized activity, security. In this sense, the break-up of the organic participation link is not initiated by expulsion from the labour market. It exists among the wage-earners' population.

The citizenship link is not safe against breaking up either. Such is the case in particular when the individuals are excessively remote (or kept away) from the institutions to obtain identity papers and being able to exercise their rights. Foreigners sometimes have difficulties in regularising their long-stay visas and are consequently in an illegal situation. The homeless are also often cut off from the administrative circuits or bounced from one department to the other without succeeding in providing all of the documents required to get help. Let us also note that in a category-based social help system, there are always some people who are excluded from the law, that is to say, people who do not match any of the categories set forth by law. Admittedly, the citizenship link may also be broken when people in distress are durably maintained, often against their own volition, in provisional structures. What good is this right if all it boils down to is emergency aid and does not enable individuals to improve their life circumstances when they are supposedly assisted or to secure access to more acceptable forms of insertion? Although emergency solutions are perennial for the recipients, they still amount to excluding other forms of help and relegation into infra-assistance status. The citizenship link can finally be considered to be broken every time the principle of citizens' equality in the face of law is blatantly defeated.

There are numerous cases of de facto discrimination in access to rights. In all modern societies, but varying from one country to another, there is still a noticeable proportion of apathetic individuals who feel detached from the society in which they live, who no longer have any sense of political belonging, who feel like aliens in the context of the tug-of-war between politicians.

Breaking-up one type of link does not automatically imply breaking-up the others. Young lovers may voluntarily break up the link with their parents (filiation link) when the latter are reluctant about their relationship and their decision to get married (elective participation link). A woman living in a closed ethnic community may decide to break up with her milieu of origin and with the tradition in order to better fit in with the conditions of modern life and to participate more actively in the working world (organic participation link). The political refugee may find in forced exile and in broken citizenship links the means to weave new social links in another country. These examples taken among so any others indicate that a break-up may remain exceptional in an individual's life but does not necessarily have a contagious effect on all of his/her social bonds.

But since the links may be broken up and since they are interlaced specifically to every person (Simmel 1908), the risk of one break-up having a snowball effect may be analysed on the basis of biographical trajectories, like a thread coming loose which irretrievably damages a cloth. Two types of cumulative break-ups may be differentiated: failed learning and statutory degradation. The former refers to the case of individuals who, as of their infancy, have met numerous difficulties associated with poverty or the deficiencies of their family and social environment and for whom life has been but a succession of break-ups. On the contrary, the latter corresponds to cases in which men and women have been struck at one stage of their lives by hardships and from which they spiralled down into failures and broken social links. But now we have reached the end of this discussion, it seems especially possible to assert that the notion of exclusion in modern societies is widely accepted to a vast extent because both basic social links, i.e. protection and recognition, are today fragilized and threatened globally, possibly questioned cumulatively, for significant fringes of the population.

4 Poverty and Exclusion in Japan: Young People and their Hopes

Yûji Genda

An undiscovered problem

The problem of social exclusion is 'an as yet undiscovered' problem. That is, it is a problem concerning people who are not even acknowledged as being socially excluded. When we think about social exclusion, we need to keep in mind that it is these forgotten people who constitute the problem of true social exclusion. Consequently, what is needed to build a society without exclusion is both acknowledgement and discovery. In other words, it is a matter of no longer ignoring those people who have been excluded by society.

How exactly then might we be able to discover this important problem that continues to be ignored by society? One way would be to take a hard look at, and change, the culture and values of society. To this end, it would be extremely valuable to apply an international comparative perspective to the problem of social exclusion.

NEETs and socially withdrawn people (*hikikomori*)

The people who are currently acknowledged in Japan as being socially excluded are those known as NEETs (Not in Education, Employment or Training) and socially withdrawn (*hikikomori*), who have been attracting attention since the beginning of the 21st century. In Japan, NEET is used to indicate unmarried youths (generally up to 35 years old), who have abandoned any plans of working (and who are therefore not even attempting to look for work). The term socially withdrawn refers to people who have been secluded within their own homes for more than one year, without any day-to-day contact with people other than their own family members.

These socially withdrawn people remained unacknowledged until the beginning of the 1990s. Similarly, the NEETs were unacknowledged, with nothing known about them until the 2000s. It was only in the 2000s that the government began to give serious thought to the existence of NEETs and socially withdrawn people. In recently released government statistics, preliminary calculations suggest that there are likely to be at least 600,000 to 700,000 NEETs and socially withdrawn people nationally. These figures include some people who are both NEETs and socially withdrawn.

At the outset, when the problem first began to be recognized, it was regarded as essentially a youth problem, but recently there have been numerous indications that this problem is also becoming widespread amongst middle-aged and older people. The parents of middle-aged and older NEETs and socially withdrawn people have to find the means to support them. However, after the death of their parents, NEETs and socially withdrawn people have difficulty meeting their living costs, and are plunged into a desperate struggle to survive.

Lack of hope

NEETs and socially withdrawn people go about their daily lives with a diverse range of feelings. It is extremely difficult to sum them up in a word. If forced to say what the widely experienced feeling is, it would most likely not be 'rage' directed at society. Rather, the characteristic that defines them (males and females alike) is precisely a sense of 'resignation' regarding not only society but also themselves. They are 'resigned' and, therefore, they say nothing. They say nothing and, therefore, they are not discovered. They are not discovered and, therefore, their social exclusion continues. The consequence of all this is that social exclusion produces a vicious circle.

In most cases, those who have given up do not even blame society. It is instead themselves that they see as the object of blame. These men and women tend to blame themselves for not being able to get on smoothly in society, seeing their own lack of abilities in matters such as personal relations as the reason for their problems. They also frequently blame their parents and families. Generally, the image of NEETs and socially withdrawn people presented in the media is that they have either little desire or aptitude for finding work or independence. However, on the basis of observations that I have garnered from families and support groups, I see a substantial portion of NEETs and socially withdrawn people as essentially possessing abundant quantities of both the desire for independence and the latent potential to achieve it.

It is, however, also true that I sensed that these men and women all lacked something in common. Just what was it that they lacked? One element that appeared to be lacking was self-confidence. At times, I also wondered whether they shared a common lack of hope: the hope to live; the hope to work; hopes concerning themselves; and hopes regarding society. I see both NEETs and socially withdrawn people lacking the hope to live for the future as well as the drive that would be required to change their current difficult circumstances.

To begin with, though, we need to ask what, exactly, are hopes. This question is also extremely problematic. Between 2005 and 2009, the Institute of Social Science, with which I am affiliated, conducted a research project entitled 'Social Sciences of Hope' looking at the relationships between society and hope. The hope study is a research theme not found anywhere else in the world, not even in France. This research is pursued with the view that knowledge of the links between society and hope might provide some hints on how to construct a society free of social exclusion.

In the course of this research into hope, social hope, for example, was thought of in terms of: *a wish for something to come true by action*. It will be difficult to bring about any improvement in the circumstances of either NEETs or socially withdrawn people by simply shouting loudly, 'Have hope!' The definition mentioned above is built on four pillars: wish, something, come true and action. That is why support, in the form of individual assistance such as appropriate education and counseling, is needed to help every individual to build up each of these pillars in their own lives.

Preventing suicide

People who have given up and people who have lost all hopes barely manage to keep going, but what is absolutely the worst situation in which they can end up? That, as we all know, is death. Tragically, Japan has one of the highest suicide rates in the world. Since 1998, Japan has recorded more than 30,000 suicides per annum. These suicides include a considerable number of elderly people who die because they are worried about illnesses, but there also appear to be significant numbers of young and middle-aged people who choose to die because they are suffering economic misery or social isolation.

Tangible counter-measures to deal with the problem of suicide are urgently needed to fight against the problem of social exclusion in Japanese society. One tangible measure that is indispensible is to erect barriers at many railway stations immediately in order to prevent falls.

When taking trains in Tokyo, announcements reporting that the train has stopped because of 'a traffic accident in which someone has been injured or killed', are practically a daily occurrence (increasing in frequency with the arrival of spring). This means that there is a seemingly endless stream of people committing suicide by jumping in front of trains. We must not, however, simply resign ourselves to these daily occurrences as the normal state of affairs. By erecting barriers to prevent falls we could bring about a considerable decline in the number of suicides resulting from people leaping in front of trains. In fact, I understand that since the implementation of preventative measures on the Marunouchi Line, which runs through Hongo Sanchōme Station near the University of Tokyo, there has not been a single incident of this kind.

Once the political decision has been taken to fund the installation of such barriers, this particular measure could be implemented immediately. This is one budget item that ought to be considered as a matter of urgency. (In fact, from 2010 onwards, the construction of barriers to prevent falls has been progressing throughout the Tokyo metropolitan area, beginning at Ebisu Station.)

Dropping out of school and long working hours

I would like to take a closer look at the actual conditions confronting Japan's NEETs. I have already referred to the fact that government statistics indicate that in Japan there are 640,000 young NEETs: not going to school, not working, not undergoing work-related training and not looking for work. However, according to my calculations, the numbers of people who find themselves in the sorts of conditions that would make them NEETs are considerably higher than is suggested by the government figures. One major reason for this is that females who 'help with household duties' are not included as NEETs in the government statistics. Amongst the people counted as 'helping with household duties' (and most of these are female), there are many who have difficulties relating to other people or who are ill. Many of them are certain to be NEETs. If we factor in those helping with household duties when we talk about NEETs, then the proportion of males and females is even. In contrast, we find that it is predominantly males who are socially withdrawn, according to the experiences of the non-profit-organizations (NPO) who provide support services to them.

Another characteristic of NEETs is that many of them are high school drop outs. It is in part for this reason that many regions in Japan are currently attempting to get high school drop outs into alternative schooling, such as part-time or distance education. As mentioned earlier, NEETs and socially withdrawn people are closely connected. There are a significant number of NEETs who were teased for their absences from school and then went on to become socially withdrawn, giving up on the idea of working.

In contrast, other young people became NEETs through a completely different series of events. This group of men and women were full-time company employees right up until the time when they became NEETs. Some of them were even more conscientious than the average employee, consistently putting in extremely long hours at work. It would be unthinkable in France, but in contemporary Japan there are still some people who work more than sixty hours per week (Genda 2003). At the beginning of the 2000s, one in four men in their thirties worked more than sixty hours a week. This means that they worked Monday to Friday from nine in the morning until after ten at night. Some of them suffered mentally and physically, eventually becoming ill. The frequency of mental illness in the workplace has become a major social problem in Japan. This situation is producing people who are exhausted by human relations, who recall excessive mental stress in communicating with people, who are panicked by the thought of having contact with others and even people who can no longer work. In reality, a significant number of young people who are NEETs have had this sort of experience of overwork.

The reproduction of poverty

Up until the beginning of the 1990s, young NEETs were primarily from families that were comparatively well off economically. In economics, the increasing tendency for more and more people to behave like those with surplus income, and indulge in leisure rather than work is called the labor supply income effect. In the period before the bubble economy collapsed, attempts to explain the circumstances that lay behind young people not looking for work were predominantly in terms of this income effect.

However, there was a big change in this tendency in the 1990s and 2000s. After I had conducted a quantitative analysis of the government statistics it became clear that it was, in fact, families lacking any surplus income, poor families, that produced young people who had abandoned hopes of working (Genda 2007).

Japan is also experiencing a clear increase in the tendency for poor families to produce young people who find it difficult to find work and therefore have no income. This has frequently been referred to as the 'reproduction of poverty'. Japan has been confronting this problem of the reproduction of poverty since the 1990s. However, the unfortunate reality in contemporary Japan is that there is still very little recognition either in society as a whole or within the government of the fact that the true nature of the NEETs problem is bound up with the problem of poverty.

The problem of social exclusion is a problem of work as well as a family problem. Formerly, there was regular cooperation by the community to help poor families. Today, however, poor families are not only in economic distress, they have also lost their links with others and are rapidly losing their links with their community.

Among the common people of Japan, there was once a custom of 'sharing a portion of profits with others'. People used to prepare extra-large portions of the evening meal, or on occasions when they were given produce by someone, they would say. 'There is far too much for us' and share it with people that they knew in the neighborhood. For the people who lived in poor regions, this practice led to harmonious human relationships, and people helped one another when they faced difficult times. When young people got up to some mischief or behaved badly in town, an adult from some part of the neighborhood would turn up and warn them to behave. In contemporary Japan, however, adults do not attempt to instruct or discipline other people's children. Indeed, children in primary school are taught that they are not to speak to adults whom they do not know. Community ties are rapidly being lost, particularly in communities with large numbers of poor families.

An alternative success story

Until quite recently the Japanese believed that the route to success was to get into one of the elite universities, and then get into a blue-chip company and continue to work there until retirement. However, this tale of success only ever applied to a limited number of people. For the majority of Japanese people, the actual paths to success were completely different from this.

Most 'ordinary' success was achieved by working diligently and unstintingly in small companies, without ever having graduated from high school (much less university), building up their experience, knowledge and skills. Then, at some point, with the backing and support of their employer (who might, for example, have arranged an introduction to a bank that would provide a loan) they end up managing their own small company; that is, they become self-employed. This sober way of life was the norm for many Japanese people (particularly for less-educated people living in rural areas). In Japan, working as a self-employed person rather than working in someone else's employ is referred to as *ikkoku ichijō no aruji ni naru* (becoming a feudal lord): i.e., being one's own boss. This idea of becoming lord over one's own domain has been an important route to success in Japan.

However, the structures that enabled less-educated people to come to have their own company and be their own boss gradually began to crumble about thirty years ago, and the numbers of people achieving success via this route has rapidly declined in Japan (Genda and Kambayashi 2002). The decline began around 1980, well before the bubble economy burst; a time when Japan was considered to be in good economic shape compared with France and other countries. According to OECD statistics, the number of countries that continued to experience a decline in the numbers of self-employed people throughout the 1980s and 1990s was not particularly large. Japan was one of the exceptions, as was France. This was a significant factor behind the closing down of pathways of social inclusion and the expansion of exclusion.

Family breakdown

Based on my research to date, I believe that there are various reasons for the decline in self-employment. Difficulties in finding the funds necessary to start new businesses were undoubtedly an important factor. A changing economic environment in which, despite being busy, the income earned by small businesses was inadequate to meet their wage obligations also hastened the demise of these businesses.

There is, however, another quite different, and even greater, problem contributing to the situation: isolation and loneliness. Evidence suggests that self-employed people increasingly feel socially isolated. Ultimately, the role played by the family is indispensible for self-employed people to avert solitude and to continue to at least survive, if not prosper, in the face of uncertain conditions. In most cases, self-employed people would not be able to keep going without the cooperation and assistance of their families. For example, a large number of the convenience stores that operate throughout Japan are run as independent franchises. The twenty-four hour nature of operations that govern convenience stores makes harmonious marital relations an essential condition for business success.

In the 1980s, Japan began to experience a variety of family problems that had not previously existed. In 1980, in a very shocking incident, a young man who had twice failed his university entrance exams bludgeoned his parents to death with a metal bat late one night. This came as a major shock, as there had seldom been incidents of parricide in Japan. In the early 1980s, the Totsuka Yacht School Incident also became a significant social issue. This incident concerned a large number of youths who had been rejected by families that could not raise them and schools that could not cope with them. They were being detained in the yacht school where many of them died as a result of corporal punishment. One of the perpetrators, Hiroshi Totsuka, was arrested, but a considerable number of politicians, parents and intellectuals vehemently argued that since these youths came from failing families they needed someone like Mr Totsuka who could deal with them severely.

At present, there are many adults in Japan who are working to support the social independence of NEETs and socially withdrawn people. A considerable number of these supporters became active in the 1980s. During an interview, a man who has been working to foster self-reliance amongst children for about thirty years said, 'Japanese families started to become strange from around the 1980s'.

Problems with self-employment and the family problems which accompany it, as well as social exclusion and related problems, all appeared in the 1980s. In other words, the family problems that had emerged well before the bubble economy collapsed have in fact become an important factor in the problem of social exclusion. It is most certainly not only a recent problem, as is suggested in the phrase 'the lost decade'.[1]

Non-permanent work

Following the Lehman Shock in the autumn of 2008 (the beginning of the Global Financial Crisis), many workers, particularly temporary workers, were dismissed. This led to the appearance of another social problem: a sharp increase in the number of homeless people. This brought to light a situation that a significant proportion of people who are employed on temporary bases find themselves in when faced with some difficulty or other: they do not have a home to which they can return nor one to which they should return. The most essential requirement for dealing with the problem of temporary work is appropriate employment measures. It is a fact especially peculiar to Japan that the generation of young people who graduated from school during the recession is more likely to end up in temporary work. In Japan, there is an overriding tendency, in both schools and corporations, to emphasize the employment of new graduates. Hence, it is very difficult for young people who can not find regular employment as new graduates to later find such work. This is why people who missed out on the one-time-only chance of becoming a regular employee as a new graduate end up with no choice but to continue as temporary employees long after their initial appointment (Genda and Kurosawa 2001; Genda, Kondo and Ohta 2008 and 2010).

In order to address the injustices faced by this generation we need labor policies capable of effecting change for temporary employees, policies that would improve the labor market and expand opportunities for the development of people's abilities. However, addressing the problems associated with current temporary work is not simply a matter of looking at employment opportunities. The problem of temporary work and insecure conditions is considerably influenced by the family environment. What can society and the government do for families that are isolated and breaking down? When third parties including governments become too deeply involved in individual families, other difficulties arise such as privacy issues which are separate from work issues. Just how much should be given to families aside from financial assistance in the form of welfare? The possibilities and limits of these types of assistance are currently being investigated anew.

In any event, many of the problems of social exclusion arise from the fact that there are people who cannot rely on their families. In contemporary Japan there are many people who no longer know the whereabouts of their families. As such, these people have been excluded from even the most basic unit of society, the family. How can they go about building a new place for themselves as a substitute for their families? This problem is being investigated as a current social exclusion issue.

Weak ties

The sociological concept of weak ties refers to relations with people who have different information, different experiences and different values from oneself. The American sociologist, Granovetter (1995), points out that people with weak ties find it easier to effect improvements in their work environment by changing jobs. The reason for this is that they can use the network of people, to which they loosely belong and who possess different knowledge from them, to obtain information that they can then use to improve their own situation. The question of whether such weak ties will spread throughout Japanese society in the future is one that will be a decisive factor in the prevention of exclusion.

Until now, Japanese society has been centered on strong family unity and equally strong unity between the employees of a company. It had been thought that being a part of this strong unity (strong ties) would guarantee future success and peace of mind. However, these days family unity is crumbling, as indicated by the fact that one in four households is a single-person household. Even in companies where new graduates would once have expected to have secure employment until retirement, it is now not uncommon to find employment adjustment practices such as early retirement and dismissals. The demise of such companies, as a result of insolvencies and mergers, and even company collapses, has already become a daily occurrence.

Hence, it will become essential for everyone in Japanese society to shift their focus from maintaining strong unity to broadening their weak ties; the loose bonds that they have with a variety of other people. Statistical analyses in Japan already indicate that the people who are successful today in changing jobs or starting up their own businesses usually have a network of weak ties (Genda 2005).

This is clearly bound up with many sociologists' remark that the issue of social class generally coincides with that of weak ties. It is well-known in sociology that people from higher social classes, who have surplus time and money, usually find it easier to form weak ties. However, social exclusion is a serious problem which, in most cases, affects people who conversely have no economic surplus, limited opportunities for movement and are regarded as coming from low social classes. How these people can set about broadening the loose bonds that they have is one of the social challenges that Japan will face from now on.

Fostering supporters

Broadening weak ties is difficult regardless of one's social class, but it is certainly not impossible. There are several hints for helping this happen. For example, the proportion of people in the workforce employed in NPOs in Japan, compared to Europe and other advanced nations, is still at an extremely low level. Bringing about an increase in the number of people engaged in activities such as those undertaken by NPOs which link people to others and lead to an increase in the weak ties within society, is likely to become increasingly important from now on. I had an opportunity to directly give advice to the Minister of Health, Labour and Welfare on this matter, stating:

> I think that it is very important for the state to provide assistance to young people who are NEETs and socially withdrawn. There is, however, another important thing to do. What is more important still is *to support young people who will themselves support these other young people*. I would like to see the government starting to apply itself now, through organizations such as NPOs, to fostering people who will support those who have difficulties with social independence.

As part of the practical policies for fostering supporters, sufficient funds need to be made available to cover the costs of this program. The way the tax system deals with donations in the future will have an important impact on this. In 2008 Japan saw the introduction of the *furusato* tax (native place tax). This is an arrangement whereby one can elect to pay a portion of the taxes that are legally owed either to the region where they were born or to a region for which they feel some sympathy or attachment. As with the idea of the native place tax, establishing new channels whereby funds can flow back in and be used to support people who are engaged in the social activity of building social independence will henceforth, I think, be vital.

The importance of international comparisons

Exactly what is social exclusion? My understanding is that there is not as yet any academic consensus on a definition of social exclusion. This is another reason why, above all, we now need to explore, rather than ignore, questions such as what kind of people we should target to foster active social inclusion and prevent exclusion, and what types of hardships and suffering they are experiencing.

The true problem of social exclusion is what has not yet been discovered. The most serious fact that people live in socially difficult conditions has not yet been discovered. That is, these problems exist unseen.

Where are socially excluded people located in Japan? How can we acknowledge them? We can continue with our efforts to discover answers to these questions while applying a comparative perspective, such as between Japan and France. This is precisely the bridge to building a society free of exclusion.

5 The Insertion of Young People into the Labor Market, and Job Quality

François Xavier Devetter

Introduction

During the 1980s and 1990s the Fordist work nexus was increasingly called into question. Stable employment under CDI contracts (open-ended), full-time contracts, and contracts whose working hours are regarded as standard, is now under the spotlight because of an increase in special types of employment (part-time, temporary, CDD [fixed-term contracts], assisted contracts, etc.). Insecurity appears to be on the increase.

The changes observed, however, do not appear to be so cut-and-dried, and the traditional and relatively stable work nexus, however, still seems to have the upper hand. The average length of service in businesses is not falling (it is even increasing [IRES 2005]), the part played by salaries in VAT calculations does not follow any strict rules of regression (and tends to be maintained), whereas general reductions in the length of the working week are improving working conditions in a certain number of cases. Furthermore, reports of a general regression do not seem pertinent and should give way to a clearer vision of increasing dualism in the labor market.

In fact, while a majority of workers continue to enjoy stable conditions, an increasing proportion of the working population is nonetheless experiencing a net degradation of its position. This dualism is very clear as far as job security is concerned: the continued dominance of CDI contracts only hides the fact that over two-thirds of new contracts are in some way insecure (IRES 2005). This dualism is just as visible with regard to working hours: the improvements enjoyed by some employees thanks to the development of tailor-made timetables or the introduction of the 35-hour week, are accompanied by an increase in atypical timetables, unpredictable hours, enforced part-time work or the maintenance of very long hours.

Not all individuals are equal in the face of this increasing insecurity, and three groups in particular seem to be affected by the increase in certain types of demanding conditions. First, women (and particularly the least qualified) continue to have the greatest difficulty entering the labor market. They are the first to be subjected to these special types of employment and high temporal availability (Devetter 2009). They continue to receive lower salaries than their male counterparts and have great difficulty achieving the same career prospects (Maruani 2003). Second, the immigrant population seems to be weakened by the fall in employment in industry and rising unemployment, and thus seems confined to the secondary sectors of the labor market, if not to certain specific jobs in the cleaning and personal service sectors. Finally, young people seem particularly vulnerable. As the erosion of the Fordist work nexus is only gradual (Devetter 2002), it is the new entrants (to the labor market) who are suffering the effects. More time spent in education leads to a longer wait (in terms of remuneration and profession) which can often seem disappointing and often lead to a feeling of loss of status. Moreover, entry into the labor market is more complex and can sometimes seem to be an 'assault course': insecurity is high, unemployment recurrent and poorly (or not at all) reimbursed, and the quality of the employment obtained mediocre. After describing the wide diversity of young people, the authors will concentrate on their initial education by highlighting the difficulties experienced by three specific groups: those without qualifications, young people from immigrant families, and salaried students (Part 1). The authors will then focus on the difficulties experienced in terms of activity and unemployment, before attempting to compare the quality of the jobs they have (Part 2). The authors will conclude by highlighting the main aspects of the consequences that increased segmentation of the labor market has on young people.

Inequality: Initial education and professional insertion

A diverse category

Defining what is meant by 'young people' is not easy: statistical sources sometimes distinguish the 15–24 year-old age bracket, and sometimes the 15–29 year-old bracket. The author is taking a rather narrow definition of youth by considering the 15–25 year-old bracket, as only this category really seems to reflect the specific aspects of job quality under discussion (see below). In France, this bracket accounted for almost 12.5 percent of the population in January 2009. The position of young people in the labor market is obviously very diverse and changes quickly with age: less than 10 percent of 15–19 year-olds is in work, and barely 50 percent of 20–24 year-olds.

As Louis Chauvel (2006) has observed, the post-1985 phenomenon of mass unemployment and a persistent unemployment rate of over 30 percent among those having left school 12 months previously, is a major set-back and could appear to represent a very specific 'generational situation'. The difficulties young people have entering the labor market is essentially a recent phenomenon dating roughly from the 1980s. Despite this significant fact, young people cannot be considered as a homogenous whole and, in fact, inequality is on the increase (see below). As Baudelot and Establet (2008) note, "increasing standards of living and education have partly (and only partly) homogenized consumption practices and standards of living. If the situation is the same for everyone, young people are far from being in the same boat".

The French situation is marked by two main phenomena: the massification of education on the one hand, and the low percentage of students who are also working on the other. If the first aspect is relatively common to all OECD countries, the second seems peculiar to France. In fact, the rapid growth in the number of people in education and the increased length of time spent in education over the past 30 years are leading to a sharp fall in the number of people in work. The proportion of students among the 18–29 year-old bracket increased by over 10 percentage points (from 12 to 22 percent) between 1990 and 2002. The situation now seems more stable and less than one-third of the under-25s are in work or looking for work. For the under-21s, the most common situation remains linked to initial education.

France stands out, however, because of her early and compact initial education system, accompanied by a very low percentage of students who are also working. This tends to have a highly adverse effect on the overall employment rate, which is particularly weak in France when compared to other European Union countries: for 15–24 year-olds it is only 30.1 percent, against 41.7 percent for the European Union (15 member states) in 2005 (CAS 2007). The 'over' unemployment of young people must therefore be put into perspective by considering the low numbers in work: the unemployment rate of

15–24 year-olds is thus 8.2 percent, against around 6 percent for the 25–60 year-old bracket.

Severe inequality in terms of initial education

If the fact of spending more time in education affects all social categories, inequality in initial education is far from having disappeared—in fact, huge differences remain with regard to socio-professional categories and national origins. Such differences concern both progress at school (results, retakes, number of years spent at school) and direction (course selection). Similarly, material status for further study remains dependent on standards of living and social origins.

Thus, a not insignificant number of young people in France still leave the education system with no qualifications: almost 17 percent of young people are affected per generation (Aliaga *et al.* 2010)—13 percent of girls and 21 percent of boys. If France is close to continental European levels, she has a much higher percentage of young people leaving the second cycle of secondary education with no qualifications than Scandinavian or East European countries. This percentage has indeed been falling for the past 30 years, mainly because the length of compulsory schooling has increased, but at the same time the situation for those without qualifications has worsened considerably when compared to qualified employees in terms of exposure to unemployment: young people without qualifications are more often than not at 'the bottom of the list'. Moreover, young people without qualifications in France are largely excluded from training programs regardless of whether they are unemployed or in work. The initial disadvantage does not therefore seem to be made up, unlike Scandinavian countries, for example (CERC 2008: 37). In fact, only 6 percent of young people without qualifications return to education (against 17 percent of young holders of a general *Baccalauréat*) and if 25 percent follow a training course outside work, such training is more often than not under the auspices of local initiatives.

At the same time, young people from the working classes and those from immigrant families (whose performance at school and choice of career path are quite specific) experience much greater difficulty. Thus, of all those who hold a doctorate, there are nine who are the offspring of executives for every one who is the offspring of a manual worker, compared to seven manual workers for one executive among those without qualifications. Similarly, young people from immigrant families spend less time at school. In fact, if the time they spend at school is more often than not marked by difficulties, their choice of career path demonstrates a clear desire for upward social mobility and a rejection of non-qualified jobs. For all that, the qualifications obtained remain poorer than for non-immigrants, thus exposing them to a more complex insertion into the labor market.

Finally, inequality in the education system is also in evidence when those students who take jobs whilst they study are taken into account. In fact, if almost half the students feel compelled to work, between 10 and 20 percent of them are affected by jobs which conflict with their studies. Such jobs often involve heavy constraints (almost 40 percent involve work in the evenings or at night) and have a clear negative impact on the student's success at university. The issue of the work/ study balance is, of course, more complex, and a significant part of the problem stems from the burden associated with the jobs taken (17 hours per week on average for French students, against less than seven for Danes). Although the insecure position of students is not the main thrust of this article, the sometimes vague limits between study and work need to be highlighted. Once again, young people from the working classes are obviously much more affected.

The insertion of young people into the labor market

Entry into the labor market is a complex process and the routes taken are always very diverse. Entry is also highly dependent on the current economic climate (IRES 2005: 65): unemployment among 15–24 year-olds has increased by over 20 percent in the space of one year, whereas employment conditions have worsened (Fondeur and Minni 2006). This dependence on the current economic climate is all the more important for those without qualifications (inertia, fixed employment costs and adjustments for salaries, etc.).

Although a not-insignificant proportion of young people (mainly those who have higher education qualifications) find it relatively easy to enter the labor market, more than one young person in three is still in an insecure job three years after starting work.

The first job is more often than not subject to a special type of contract. For young people of the 2004 generation, only 30 percent get their first job under CDI (23 percent of those without qualifications, and 57 percent of those with qualifications from national engineering schools). Women are highly affected by part-time contracts, which

Figure 5.1: The situation of young people three years after finishing their initial education

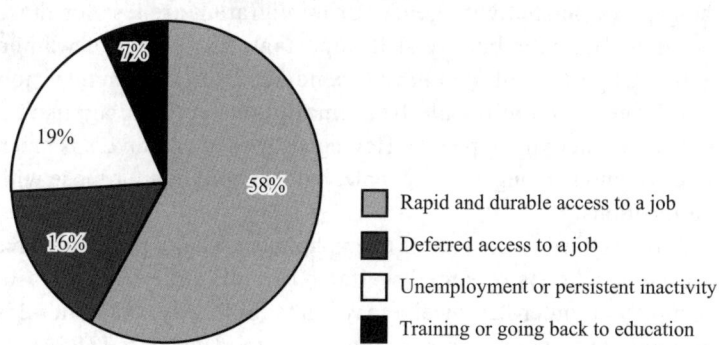

Source: CEREQ, *Génération 2004*

affect almost one woman in two without qualifications. Those with no or few qualifications tend towards assisted and temporary contracts, yet CDD contracts are common regardless of the level of education. Studies by CEREQ (*Centre d'Etudes et de Recherche sur les Qualifications*, The (French) Centre for Study and Research into Qualifications) paint a poor picture of the situation of young people three years after finishing their initial education:

The difficulties experienced by young people as they seek to enter the labor market can be divided into two main themes: high job insecurity linked with reduced social welfare; and access to low-quality jobs. Job insecurity and instability thus seem particularly pronounced for young people. Not only is the unemployment rate much higher than for older employees, but the proportion of insecure jobs is also very high: 34 percent of the under-29s, against 9 percent of 30–49 year-old employees. Periods of unemployment at the beginning of their working lives are longer (and more frequent than in Germany for example), and unemployment is a common occurrence for young people (54 percent face unemployment during the first three years of their working lives, and 33 percent are unemployed for more than six months).

For all that, insecurity is not the same for everyone: temporary work mainly affects men, whereas part-time work largely affects women. Temporary work is also more common among young people from immigrant families. Special forms of contract, however, are only a mediocre bridge towards stable employment. Rapid access to a permanent job affects only 34 percent of those with no qualifications. The gaps associated with gender or immigration are less for those with qualifications but are still important: 55 percent of women against 61 percent of men have a rapid access to a permanent job, 49 percent of young people from immigrant families, against 59 percent of other young people. Having a string of employers is much more common among young people, but less common for those with qualifications.

More exposed to the risk of unemployment, young people receive much lower levels of social welfare. In fact, only 43 percent of unemployed under-25s receive payments. Similarly, the under-25s were unable to claim the *revenue minimum d'insertion* (RMI, or minimum integration income). The RSA (*revenu de solidarité active*, or active solidarity income) which replaced it is now available to young people, but the conditions are so strict that the number of potential beneficiaries will be severely limited. Both of these factors combine to explain the over-representation of young people in the poor sections of the population (this concerns more than 800,000 people aged 18–24, and the instance of poverty is at its highest for this age group: 18.6 percent of women and 16.4 percent for men, against 11.5 percent for the population as a whole). Young people do, however, benefit from the numerous mechanisms of assisted employment benefit (40 percent of the under-26s in work; Fondeur and Minni 2006).

These insertion difficulties are fairly well known, but it would appear that there are similar disadvantages with regard to job quality, as will be shown in the second part of this chapter.

The over-representation of degraded jobs

How can the quality of a job be assessed and degraded jobs identified?

Since the 1990s, various avenues of thought have been explored in an attempt to define and measure job quality. The European Union gave particular impetus to this field of research after the Lisbon summits of March 2000. This innovative approach produced some comparative analyses between national systems of employment (Davoine and Ehrel 2006) and opened the issue to wider debate. Measuring job quality was at the heart of ILO-backed studies on the notions of 'decent work' (Bescond *et al.* 2004; Anker *et al.* 2003; and

Ghai 2003) and 'adequate work'. Other studies went into more detail, notably within the framework of European trades unions (Leschke and Watt 2008).

Studies aiming to measure job quality on an individual (rather than national) basis appear to be fewer in number. Some studies are based mainly on subjective appreciation resulting from surveys asking one specific question relating to the satisfaction of the job held (Afsa 2008), whereas others attempt to construct a typology or indicator of job quality based on specific characteristics declared by the employee—such was the approach adopted by Luc Cloutier (2009) in Canada, for example. It is this second approach which interests us here.

According to the authors, job quality is thus based on two complementary ideas:
- First, it seems that the quality of a job is the object of specific conventions. A given job is evaluated against a 'job norm' which could be defined as the majority situation (statistically speaking) which is symbolically regarded as legitimate (see Devetter 2002). In this sense it constitutes the type of job 'which seems appropriate', and attempts can be made to define any variations from this 'norm'.
- Second, it is essential that the convention of job quality be regarded as multi-faceted. Defining these facets is the first obstacle and is partly the result of arbitrary choices, which could reveal differing ideas as to what is meant (or should be meant) by job quality. If the quality of a job is 'intrinsically' multi-faceted, the actual choice of variables and dimensions will differ according to the indicators. For all that, within the different 'conventions' of job quality, some elements strike the authors as being sufficiently robust, such as remuneration, job security (also called 'stability'), working conditions, and a group of factors associated with the resources required to perform the job.

In their definition of 'job quality' the authors have included aspects which are more concerned with the 'work nexus' (which touches on *production* and refers to working conditions, work organization, relations with colleagues, managers, etc.[1]) and aspects linked to the 'job nexus' (which touches on *protection associated with the job*, and refers in particular to job security[2]) (Paugam 2000). In the authors' analysis, the work nexus is explored mainly through the concepts of 'working conditions' and 'work resources', whereas the job nexus is understood as 'remuneration' and 'stability' (see Figure 3.2 and Appendix 1). These two aspects are very distinct, but can be analyzed together here so that what the authors call job quality can be studied as a whole. The overlap between these two different aspects will allow the authors to analyze situations where difficulties (or resources) combine or compensate each other in both the work and job nexus.

Identifying degraded jobs
The four aspects identified by the authors appear to be closely linked; they sometimes balance each other out (a high salary compensating for difficult working conditions) as compensation theory tends to confirm (Smith 1776, Rosen 1974), yet the unfavorable aspects can combine in certain jobs or sectors of the population, according to how the labor market is segmented (Piore and Doeringer 1971). A comparison based on a multitude of different characteristics makes inequality less visible.

At the same time, constructing a composite indicator bringing these various dimensions together into a single measure seems tricky: which weighting is to be retained, and how can an improvement in working conditions be measured against a fall in job insecurity? If these various aspects join together well to constitute job quality, measuring them on a single axis requires the elaboration of strong and frequently subjective hypotheses. That is why the authors are not seeking to measure job quality (understood as an average of different variables, which would be highly dependent on weighting), but are proposing to identify (using an indicator) the constraints which weigh heavily on a job and then to isolate those jobs which combine the most constraints (which will be called 'degraded jobs' here) to identify the most disadvantaged sectors of the labor market.

To construct this indicator, the authors refer to the data published in the *Enquête Conditions de Travail 2005* (Working conditions survey for 2005 or CdT). There are four successive stages (see Appendix 1):
- First: identification of the variables that can be used to describe each of the four aspects of job quality selected by the authors (remuneration, job security, working conditions, resources). Job security, for example, will be considered through type of contract, expressed (or otherwise) fear of losing one's job, working full-time or part-time, etc. (column 1 in the table shown in Appendix 1).

- Second: counting the number of difficult aspects declared by the employee. This is a first 'composite' measurement based more often than not on five variables which are different but from the same sphere: for example, physically, psychologically or temporally difficult aspects are grouped together under 'working conditions'.
- Third: identification of those employees who are the most exposed to a particular constraint. The threshold used to separate individuals has always been selected so as to isolate the 15–25 percent least well-off employees (columns 2 and 3 in the table shown in Appendix 1). The authors are therefore considering each of these four major aspects of job quality in terms of the negative deviation from a 'norm' which they will later call a 'constraint' or 'constraining factor'.[3]
- Finally: classification of employees according to the number of 'constraining factors' endured (between 0 and 4). A 'degraded job' is thus defined as one which combines three or four major constraints (last line of the table in Appendix 1).

Do young people occupy a specific position with regard to job quality?

So what does this indicator tell us about young people?

First, it highlights that young people are indeed much more frequently affected by degraded jobs. Almost 20 percent of the under-20s and almost 15 percent of the 20–25s have jobs which combine three or four major constraints. This proportion then decreases sharply to stabilize at around 5 percent for all age groups. So although the under-25s represent barely 9 percent of all employees, they occupy more than 20 percent of degraded jobs.

This can obviously be explained by the fact that young employees largely have no or few qualifications, and that proportionally they are more likely than their elders to belong to the socio-professional class of employees and manual workers which accounts for most degraded jobs. Thus, 95 percent of 15–20 year-olds and 76 percent of the 20–25s are either employees or manual workers, whereas these categories represent just over 50 percent of all employees. Moreover, young people are largely over-represented in certain professions which offer very poor-quality jobs. The classic example is the fast-food industry which seems to be very low down the scale in terms of job quality, according to Cazes and Missègue (2001). For all that,

Figure 5.2: Proportion of employees based on total number of constraints

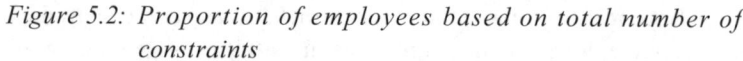

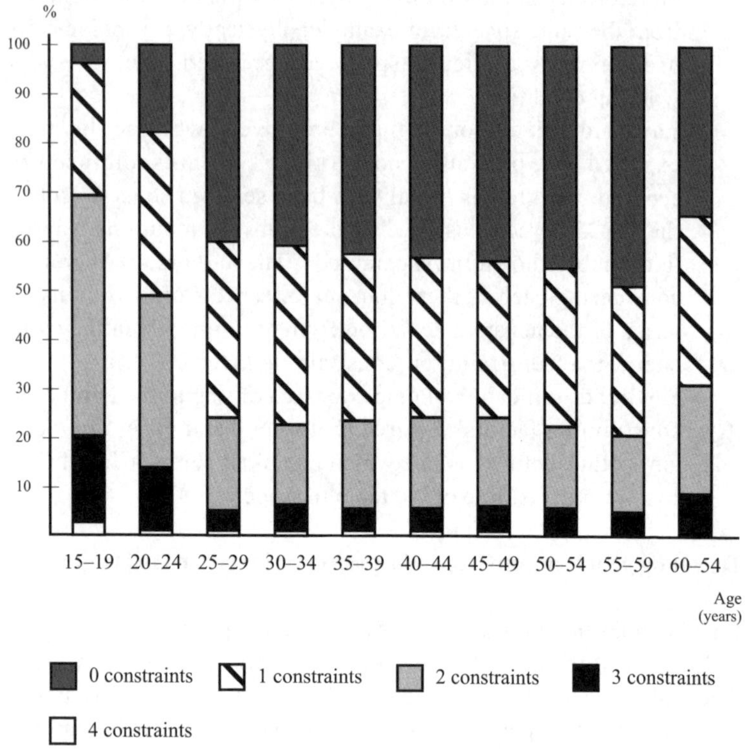

■ 0 constraints ◨ 1 constraints ▨ 2 constraints ■ 3 constraints
☐ 4 constraints

Source: *Enquête conditions de travail 2005.* Field: All employees
Note. Example: 20 percent of 15–19 year-old employees combine 3 or 4 constraints.

when the proportion of degraded jobs within each socio-professional class is examined, it appears that age still continues to play a certain role for manual workers and, to a lesser extent, for employees. More than 20 percent of manual workers under 25 years-old are affected, against around 8 percent for the next age brackets (14 percent and 10 percent respectively for employees). In industry, a certain number of constraints (notably physical constraints) thus decrease with age. This is less visible in service industries (Gollac and Volkoff 2005).

This professional situation can also be observed with regard to gender: the level of degraded jobs decreases sharply with age for men, but much less so for women. This difference is particularly noticeable for certain difficulties such as monotony.

Figure 5.3: The proportion of employees declaring that their work is very often, or often, monotonous

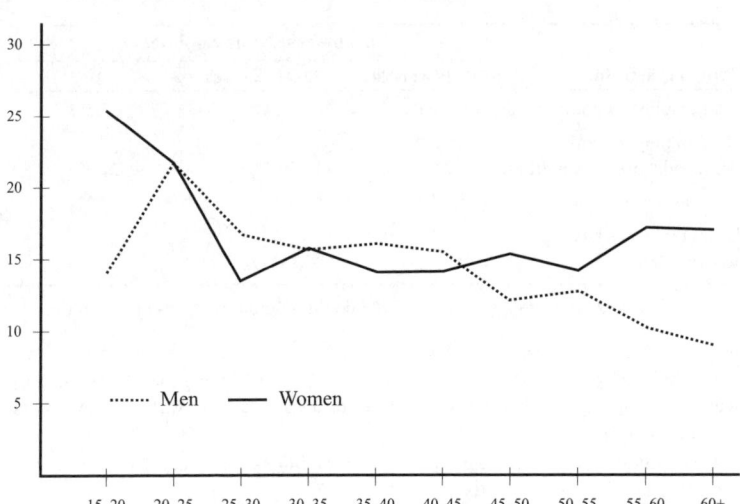

Source: *Enquête conditions de travail 2005.* Field: all employees

Some aspects of job quality are, however, more linked to age than others. On the one hand, young people are characterized by low pay and greater job insecurity, and not least by working conditions which are noticeably more difficult. On the other hand, they have more resources at their disposal than their older colleagues (assistance from colleagues or superiors, sufficient equipment and time, etc.).

The low quality of jobs held by young people cannot be explained solely by age. Variables linked to qualifications or seniority, as stressed by various analyses, must also be considered, 'all things being equal'. Thus the characteristic features of those who have recently joined the labor market are thus very similar to all new recruits (Fondeur and Minni 2006). The logistic regression carried out using the degraded job as the base (not reproduced here), stresses that seniority and gender play a greater role than age. For this aspect, only the youngest (the under-25s) show a significant effect.

The difficulties experienced by young people are particularly great for those from immigrant families (notably from the Maghreb): lower-skilled jobs, more degraded working conditions, greater insecurity and a more frequent sense of lack of status, which feeds a feeling of widespread discrimination (Okba and Lainé 2004).

Table 5.1: Proportion of employees and manual workers subject to each type of constraint according to age

Type of constraint	Manual workers and employees		
	15–19 year-olds	20–24 year-olds	All
% of employees poorly paid	90%	54%	35.5%
% of employees with degraded working conditions	31.5%	30.5%	27.5%
% of insecure employees	56%	53%	33%
% of employees having few resources	12%	15%	22%

Source: *Enquête conditions de travail 2005*. Field: manual workers and employees.

Notes:
1. Example. 90 percent of 15–19 year-old employees are among the 25 percent least well-paid employees. This is also the case for 35.5 percent of (all) employees and manual workers.
2. For definitions of low pay, degraded working conditions, job insecurity and resources, see paragraph 2.1 and Appendix 1.

Conclusion

Comparing different age groups is always a complex issue as various factors (seniority, qualifications, etc.) can interfere with the effect of age *per se*. If it is thus unequivocal that insecurity, unemployment and degraded jobs notably affect employees under-25 years-old to a much greater extent, a more balanced approach is advisable when linking this situation to a generational effect. Moreover, comparing young people from the 2000s to those of previous generations is not easy, and produces ambiguous results.

The 1990s were the backdrop to significant changes: the historic fall in non-qualified jobs began to reverse in 1993–1994. Those without qualifications, frequently faced with poor quality jobs, have been increasing for 15 years. This phenomenon is occurring at a time when the active population is acquiring more and more qualifications and where the concept of equal opportunities seems to be almost a consensus (even though some critics are emerging: see François Dubet's contribution in this work). These three factors are thus highly contradictory and the cause of much social tension.

So for those just joining the labor market, access to senior positions is more complex: salaries are lower, working conditions are marked by a greater number of difficulties, and the jobs available enjoy lower legal and social recognition. The current generations of young people have much lower career prospects (Chauvel 2006) and the risk of a loss of status is much greater for them than for previous generations (even though the means of measuring this is still a complex issue [Maurin 2009]).

Above all, the act of starting work is marked by high levels of inequality: between 1979 and 1999 when inequality was in retreat for most age groups, the inter-decile ratio for 25–29 year-olds increased markedly from 2.7 to 3.1 (Chauvel 2006). The difficulties of entering a stable situation are thus largely centered on specific groups, such as young people from immigrant families.

Appendix 1

Table showing the parameters and thresholds used to build the indicator.

Table 5A1: *The parameters and thresholds used to build the indicator.*

Variables	Measurement	The 4 factors which constitute job quality
Salary measured from one variable: SALRED: Net monthly salary	Variable SALAIRE = 0 if over 1,073 Euros 1 if below 1,073 Euros (Threshold = 25 % percent of the most well-paid)	*Salary* SALARY = 1 if below 1,073 Euros (Threshold = 25 %)
Physical difficulty based on difficulties studied in the CdT: CWDEBOU: Spending long periods standing CWDEPLA: Long and frequent trips on foot CWLETR: Reading small print CWLOURD: Carrying or moving heavy objects CWMINUS: Examining tiny objects CWMVT: Painful or tiring movement CWPOSTU: Other difficult or tiring posture CWVIB: Enduring jolts or vibration CWVISO: Brief visual or audio signals, unexpected or difficult to detect CWVUE: Not looking away from one's work	Variable PENPHYSIK = 0 if fewer than six difficulties experienced 1 if six or more difficulties (Threshold = 19 % of the salaried population with at least 6 physical difficulties out of 10)	
Psychological difficulty, based on 6 difficulties studied in the CdT: TENSION1: Experiencing tense situations, when in contact with the public DETRESSE: Being in contact with people in distress TENSION2: Experiencing tense situations when dealing with superiors TENSION3: Experiencing tense situations when dealing with colleagues CALMER: Having to calm people down at work	Variable PENPSYCHO = 0 if fewer than four difficulties experienced 1 if at least four (Threshold = 24 % of the salaried population with at least 4 psychological difficulties out of 6)	

AGRESVER: Being exposed to verbal abuse

Time-related difficulties, based on 5 difficulties studied in the CdT:
PREMOIS: Knowing the hours you will have to work during the following month
TTTEP: Average number of hours per work, main job (regular)
PERIODE: Having several different working periods during the day
DIMANC: Working Sundays
NUITC or SOIRC: Working nights (midnight to 5am) or evenings (8pm-midnight)

Variable DISPONIB =
0 if fewer then 3 difficulties experienced
1 if at least 3.
(Threshold = 12 % of the salaried population with at least 3 time-related difficulties out of 5)

Exposure to professional risk, based on 5 risks studied in the CdT:
SECACCID: Risk of injury or accident
SECFUPOU: Breathing fumes or dust
SECINFEC: Being exposed to the risk of infection
SECROUT: Risk of traffic accident
SECTOXNO: Being in contact with dangerous products

Variable SECURITE =
0 if fewer than 4 difficulties experienced
1 if at least 4
(Threshold = 15 % of the salaried population with at least 4 difficulties out of 5)

Unhealthy or unsafe working environment based on 8 items identifed in the CdT:
HYGCHAUD: High temperature
HYGCOUR: Draughts
HYGFROID: Low temperature
HYGHUMI: Dampness
HYGODEUR: Bad smells
HYGSAL: Dirt
HYGSANI: Lack of, or bad sanitary facilities
HYGVUE: Lack of view to the outside

Variable HYGIENEB =
0 if fewer than five difficulties experienced
1 if at least five
(Threshold = 18 % of the salaried population with at least 6 health-related difficulties out of 8)

Working conditions
WORKING CONDITIONS = 1 if at least 2 of the 5 types of difficulty
(Threshold = 24 %)

Table 5A1: Continued

Variables	Measurement	The 4 factors which constitute job quality
Job security, based on 4 variables:	Variable INSTABLE =	*Job security*
Legal status of contract (based on two variables):	0 if fewer than two types of insecurity experienced	INSECURE = 1 if at least two types of difficulty (Threshold = 25 %)
CONTRA: Type of employment contract	1 if at least two.	
TITC: Status of public sector employees and local authorities	(Threshold = 25 % of the salaried population with at least two insecurity-related difficulties out of 4)	
Subjective approach:		
CRAINTE: Fear for one's job		
Opportunity to learn new things:		
NOUVELLE: Learning new things		
Perceived ability to 'last out':		
TENIR: Feeling able to do the same job until the age of 60 or retirement		
Resources to carry out the work correctly, based on 7 items identified in the CdT:	Variable MOYENS: 0 if at least four resources 1 if fewer than four resources	
CORRTAN: Enough time	(Threshold: 17 % of the salaried population with fewer than four resources)	
CORRINF: Clear, sufficient information		
CORRCOP: Possibility of cooperation		
CORRCOL: Collaborators (or colleagues) in sufficient numbers		
CORRMAT: Sufficient and appropriate equipment		
CORRFORM: Sufficient and appropriate training		
CORRLOG: Sufficient and appropriate computer and information management programs		

Possible assistance (based on 4 items form the CdT):
AIDCHEF: Possibility of assistance from superiors
AIDCOLL: Possibility of assistance from colleagues
AIDAUTR: Possibility of assistance from others in the company
AIDEXT: Possibility of assistance from people outside the company

Legal recognition:
CHSCT: Establishment covered by a health and safety committee (CHSCT)

Information on risks:
RISK: Having received information about the possible risks of the work to health and safety during the previous 12 months

Work groups:
COLLECT: Opportunity to discuss together issues relating to the organization and functioning of the workplace

Variable AIDES:
0 if at least one source
1 if no assistance possible
(Threshold: 15 % of the salaried population with no assistance)

Variable CHSCT:
0 if CHSCT present
1 if not

Variable RISK:
0 if information received
1 if not

Variable COLLECT:
0 if yes
1 if no

Resources
RESOURCES = 1 if at least 3 resources lacking (Threshold = 18 %)

TOTAL: QUALITY = SALARY + CDT + INSECURE + RESOURCES
Degraded job if QUALITY $\geq$ 3

6 Changes and Problems in the Youth Labor Market in Japan

Yuki Honda

Introduction

This chapter discusses changes and problems in the youth labor market in Japan. Four main points are discussed. First, the changes in the employment situation and working conditions of young people since the early 1990s are described. Second, the discourses about youth associated with these changes are examined. Third, the causes for the rapid change in the youth labor market in Japan are explained. Finally, some countermeasures necessary to improve the employment situation and working conditions of young people are proposed.

The recent youth labor market in Japan is characterized by its strong 'dualism', which refers to the great gap between regular and non-regular workers. Since the early 1990s, the number of regular workers has reduced while that of non-regular workers has significantly increased among young people. This has resulted in both regular and non-regular workers experiencing ever-deteriorating working conditions.

The changing trend in the youth labor market has been described through the keywords 'freeter' and 'NEET'. These terms have served to blame young people for their own employment problems.

At least three causes of the rapid change in the Japanese youth labor market can be discerned: first, the 'unfortunate coincidence' between economic fluctuations and the uneven age composition of Japan's population; second, 'irreversible global long-term changes' such as the transformation of industrial structures and changing labor demands caused by the globalization of the economy; and last, the 'relationship between education and work peculiar to Japan'.

Several measures are indispensable to reducing problems in the Japanese youth labor market, such as improving the vocational relevance of school education, abolishing the convention of periodic blanket recruitment of new graduates, reducing the wage and career opportunity gap between regular and non-regular workers, expanding opportunities for inexpensive public vocational training, and opening opportunities for vocational guidance and counseling to a wider range of young people, including graduates.

Through such measures, the Japanese youth labor market might be changed to a more flexible, fair, and open one. To leave the present situation unchallenged will inflict major damage on individuals' well-being and the sustainability of Japanese society.

Changes in the employment situation and working conditions of young people

The recent youth labor market in Japan is characterized by its strong 'dualism', a reference to the great gap between regular and non-regular workers (OECD 2009). The term 'regular workers' implies permanent, although not necessarily lifetime, full-time workers. 'Non-regular workers' consist of part-time workers, temporary workers, contracted workers, and dispatched workers. Since the early 1990s, the number of regular workers has reduced while that of non-regular workers has substantially increased among young people (Figure 6.1). In 2007, more than 30 percent of workers aged 15–24 were in various forms of non-regular work. This change has resulted in both regular and non-regular workers experiencing ever-deteriorating working conditions.

First, non-regular workers are subject to job insecurity and poverty. The fact that the path leading from non-regular to regular employment opportunities is narrow has a negative effect on future prospects for young non-regular workers and increases their levels of anxiety and despair. Not only is their employment situation unstable, but their wages are also extremely low compared to regular workers (Figure 6.2), and most of them are trapped in low-skilled, dead-end jobs. Moreover, they are constantly required to transfer from one workplace to another, which makes it difficult to build good relationships with colleagues.

Although about one out of three young workers is faced with such difficult living conditions, Japanese society as a whole seems to be rather peaceful compared to, for example, France and Korea, where labor problems have led to riots. This is only because many young non-regular workers in Japan are able to rely on their parents' incomes and savings for the present. Seventy to eighty percent of young non-regular workers live with their parents. Their parents' financial support temporarily buries the problems of non-regular

Figure 6.1: Change in the number of young people (aged 15–34)

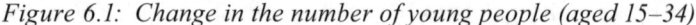

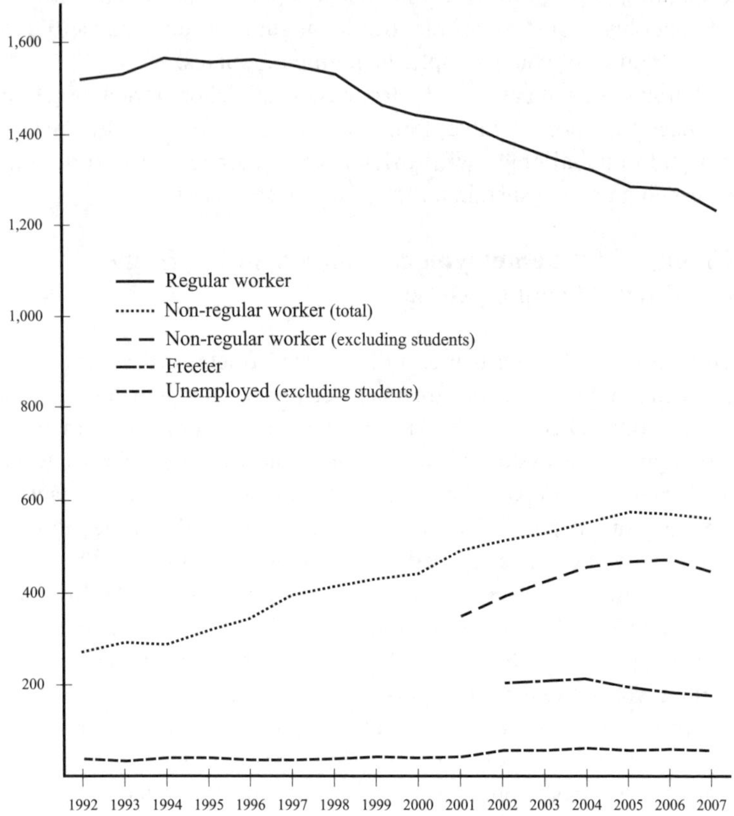

Source: Ministry of Internal Affairs and Communications, *Labor Force Survey*

workers; however, this situation will not prevail for long. In the next few decades, after their parents' demise, low-wage workers will no longer be able to sustain their living standards. It is estimated that a relatively large proportion of these workers will have no way of earning a living and will be reliant on public welfare protection. Japanese society will have to address this problem sooner or later. Already today, those who cannot rely on parents are experiencing extreme hardship.

Non-regular jobs are so unstable that workers may lose their jobs simply by getting sick and taking a week's leave from work. This is particularly evident in the case of day laborers, who earn very little

Figure 6.2: Distribution of annual income (age total)

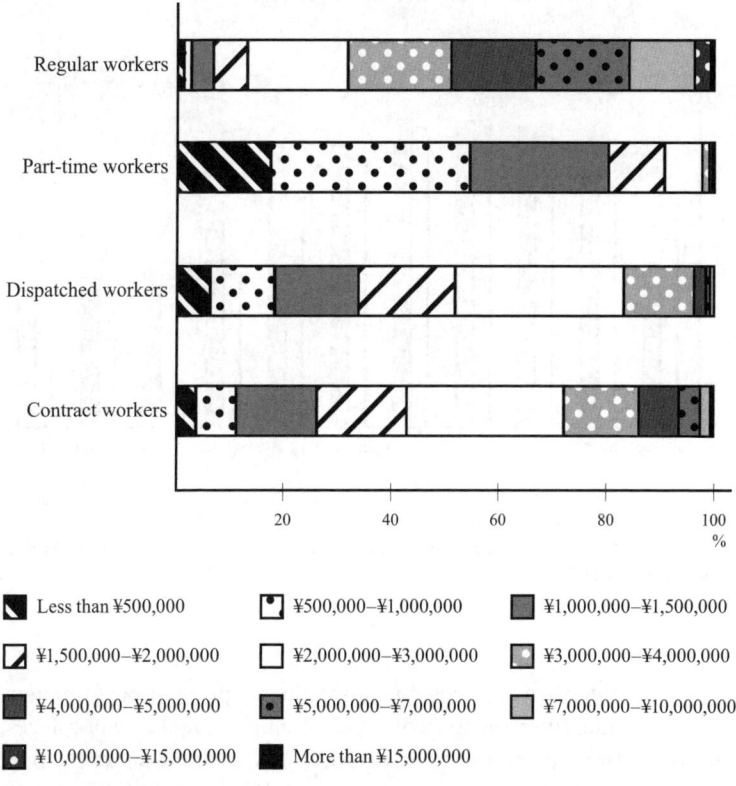

Source: Ministry of Health, Labor and Welfare, *2008 White Paper*.

money; their absence from work for just one week could lead to their inability to pay rent. As a consequence, they might lose their residence and become homeless or a 'net café refugee', i.e., someone who sleeps in internet cafés every night.

However, even regular workers are not as secure or privileged as they were previously. The period 1993–2004 was marked by severe cutbacks in the hiring of regular workers. As a result, the average workload for regular workers has increased, and they are now also required to manage the increased number of non-regular workers. Although working hours have increased along with workloads (Figure 6.3), they are no longer promised the seniority-based wage rises that previous generations had enjoyed.

Figure 6.3: *Rate of male regular workers who work more than 60 hours per week (according to age)*

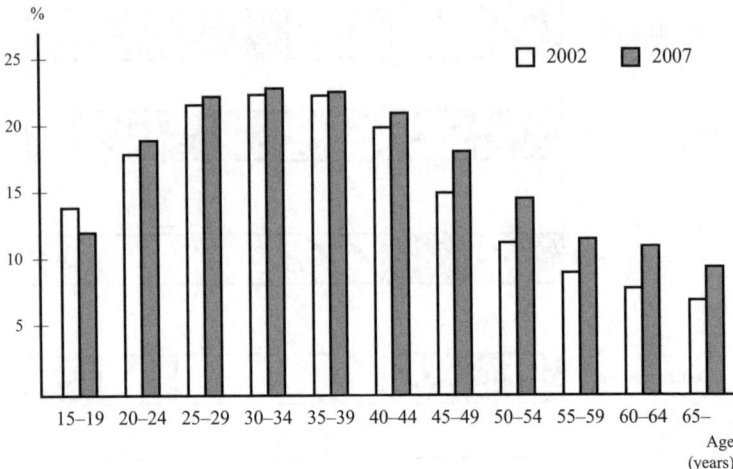

Source: Ministry of Internal Affairs and Communications, *Basic Survey of Employment Structure 2007*

Due to a number of issues, including the adoption of performance-based pay, the diversification of types of employment in workplaces, and reductions in hiring young people from the same age group, young regular workers find it increasingly difficult to develop a sense of camaraderie with their colleagues. Instead, with an increasing number of antagonistic relationships, more workers have begun to experience mental health issues (Figure 6.4). There are, of course, differences among regular workers' statuses according to their respective company size and business policies.

This dualism, in which both regular and non-regular young workers suffer from the stark contrasts in conditions, can be metaphorically described as 'the concurrence of a white hell and a black hell'. There is a paradoxical relation between regular and non-regular workers; non-regular workers function as a 'buffer' that helps to maintain the employment security of regular workers, while, at the same time, the low wages and employment insecurity of the non-regular workers are deteriorating the working conditions of regular workers. Thus, the dualism within the youth labor market itself fuels a vicious circle.

Figure 6.4: Number of claims for workers' compensation insurance according to the type of illness

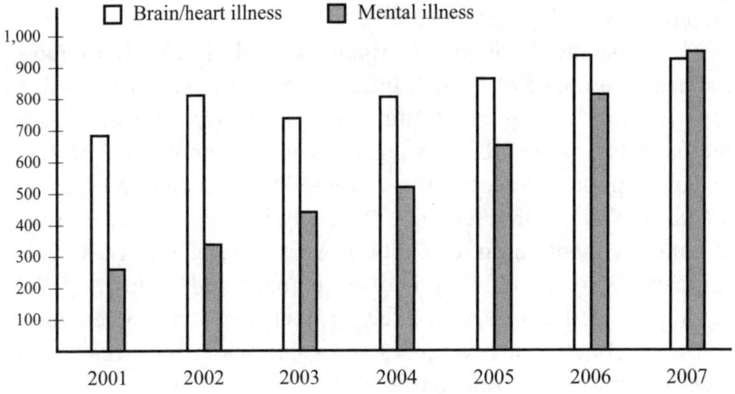

[Bar chart showing Brain/heart illness and Mental illness claims from 2001 to 2007]

Source: Ministry of Health, Labor and Welfare

Changing discourses on young people

The second part of this chapter discusses changes in the discourses on young people over the past few decades. One of the significant trends in young workers has been described with the term 'freeter', a term coined by an editor of a job advertisement magazine, which refers to freelance, part-time workers (Honda 2005). When the term freeter emerged in the late 1980s, it originally connoted 'a vigorous and free youth'. By the late 1990s, however, it had come to mean 'a lazy and dependent youth'. Moreover, in the early 2000s, the meaning changed again to 'a young person who is pathologically going nowhere'. This changing image of the word freeter is inseparable from a trend to blame young people for their own employment problems.

Similarly, the term 'NEET', an acronym for young people who are 'Not in Education, Employment, or Training', has spread rapidly and widely throughout Japan since 2004 (Honda et al. 2006). The Japanese usage of the word NEET is different from that in Britain, where the term originated. In Japan, the official definition of NEET excludes unemployed youths seeking a job. This provoked an image of a NEET as 'a young person lacking the motivation to work'. The common idea that most Japanese NEETs are born in middle class families instead of working class or poor families has exacerbated the stereotype. The definition of NEET also includes a broad age group from 15 to 34, the result of which is that estimates of the NEET population amounted to more than 800,000. This aggravates the gloomy view of Japanese youths.

The mass media played an important role in the diffusion of the negative image of NEETs in Japan. Five characteristics can be identified in the representations of NEETs in the Japanese mass media. First, being NEET is regarded as a psychological problem of young people. Second, the commonality between NEETs and '*hikikomori*'—a term referring to 'socially isolated' people who stay at home, without going to school or work—are emphasized. Third, the parents' responsibility is often emphasized. Fourth, NEETs are stigmatized as losers, and the term has developed a derogatory character. Finally, many causes and solutions to the situation are asserted with no scientific bases.

In contrast to the negative term NEET, the term '*ningenryoku*', or 'human competence', is used to focus on the expected positive aspects of young people. From the late 1990s, human competence has been frequently used in the mass media and policy papers. The term human competence is interconnected with the personal and emotional traits of a person, such as communication skills and problem solving capabilities. As a result, many people have come to believe that most of the young people's problems can be resolved by nurturing their human competence.

However, empirical data on NEETs conflicts with these popular understandings of young people. Data shows that the popular conception of NEETs as simply youths lacking the will to work is incorrect. Most NEETs are either willing to work or have no need to work immediately, engaging in various activities within or without their families. Although some NEETs are inactive, this cannot be attributed solely to mental problems. Rather, social factors such as the experience of bullying in schools and workplaces, dropping out of school, loss of parents, and similar factors must be taken into account. A major problem is that the use of the word NEET has spread mistaken beliefs about the current state of young people.

Causes of the change in youth labor market

The third point to be discussed in this chapter is the causes and origins of the rapid change in the youth labor market in Japan. Three causes can be discerned.

First is the 'unfortunate coincidence' between economic fluctuation and the uneven age composition of the Japanese population. There are two huge age cohorts within the Japanese population: one is the first generation of baby boomers born in the late 1940s and the other is the second generation of baby boomers born in the early 1970s. During the 'bubble economy' around 1990, Japanese companies recruited a large number of second generation baby boomers as regular workers. After the bubble burst they became heavy burdens for Japanese companies, as labor laws made it very difficult to dismiss regular workers. Moreover, during the 1990s, the first generation baby boomers were reaching their 50s and their labor costs were peaking. This double pressure on companies meant that they refrained from recruiting new young regular workers, relying instead on non-regular workers. Today, the age imbalance of the working population is gradually improving. However, the employment situation and working conditions of the so-called 'lost generation', those born in the late 1970s and through the 1980s, continue to be a critical issue.

The second reason for the change in working styles is the transformation of industrial structures and labor demands in response to the globalization of the economy. These are irreversible global long-term changes. In every developed country, the industrial structure has been shifting from manufacturing to service industries (Figure 6.5). The manufacturing industry is not only shrinking in quantity but also transforming its quality from mass production to small-lot multiple production. These industrial trends stimulate growing demand for non-regular workers, who can be mobilized 'just in time' at reduced labor costs. This continuously developing transition is observed in almost all developed countries, posing grave global challenges.

The third factor is 'the peculiar relationship between education and work in Japan', which has worsened the situation for young workers. Japanese schools have been reluctant to match their education to occupational demands (Figure 6.6), and the periodic blanket recruitment of new graduates is a custom peculiar to Japan. The lack of vocational relevance of school education deprives youth of both market value and the power to bargain with employers. The custom of periodic blanket recruitment of new graduates means that young people who do not find a job upon graduation run into difficulty trying to enter a favorable labor market later. I consider this 'peculiar relationship between education and work in Japan' to

Figure 6.5: Shift in the rate of workers in the manufacturing industry (by country)

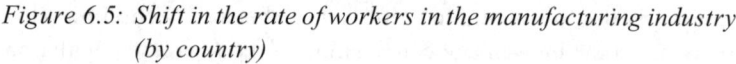

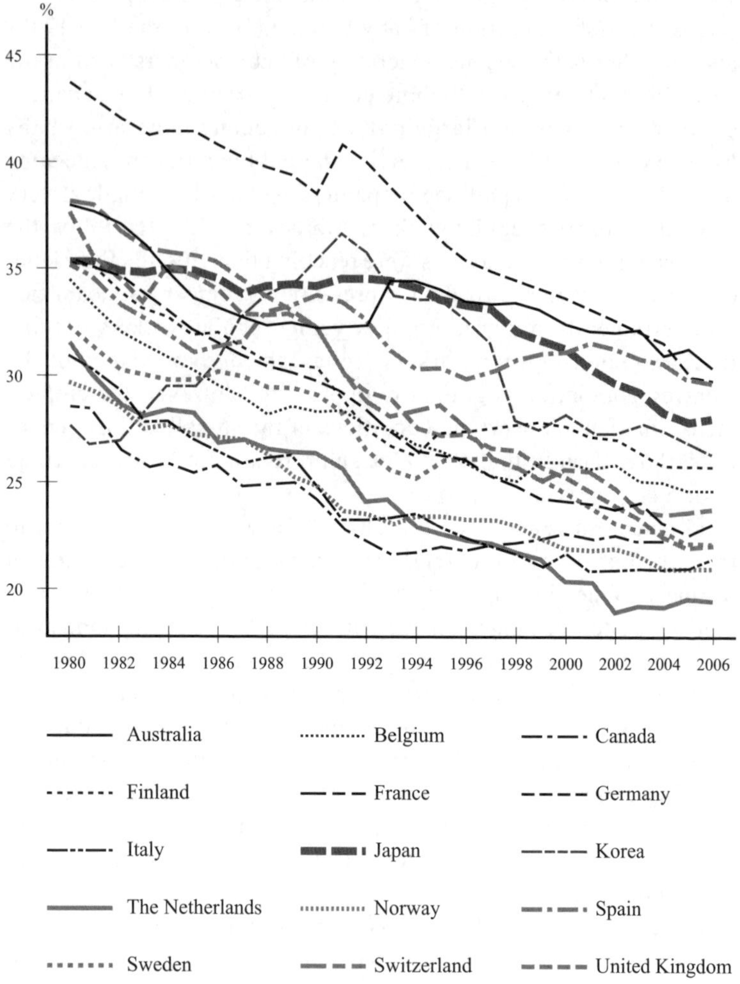

Source: OECD, *Labor Force Statistics*

be the most urgent of the issues facing young people in Japan; one that must be and can be changed. This leads us to the final part of our discussion: the measures required to improve the employment situation and working conditions of young people in Japan.

Figure 6.6: Number of youth who feel that they have acquired vocational skills through education (according to educational background)

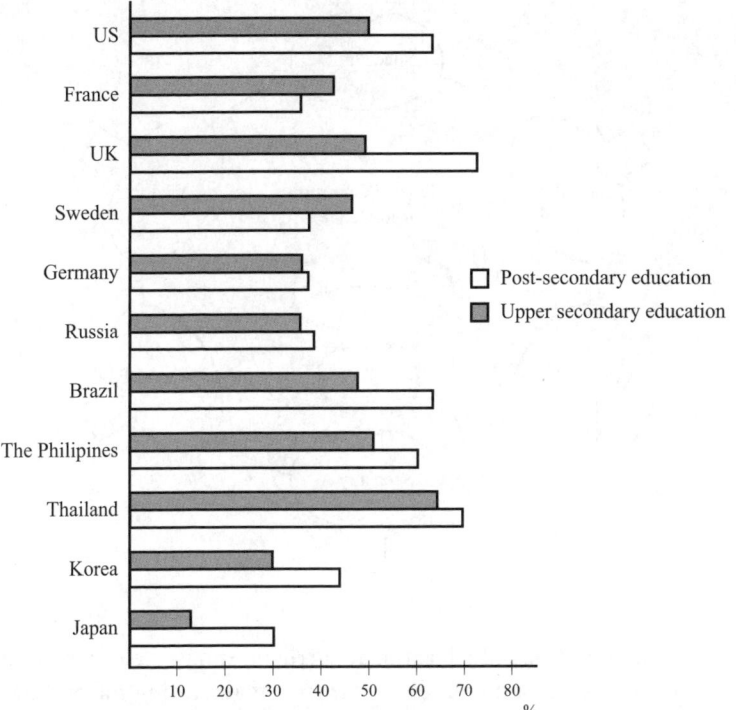

Source: Cabinet Office, *The 6th World Youth Survey*, 1998

Necessary measures

Several measures are necessary to change 'the peculiar relationship between education and work in Japan' and to improve the situation of Japanese youth.

First, we need to make education match companies' occupational demands. In other words, the vocational relevance of the educational contents of schools and universities must be improved. In particular, the number of technical and professional high schools, which is too small in Japan, should be increased. In order to cope with rapidly changing technology and the global economic environment, the

Figure 6.7: Model of "flexpeciality"

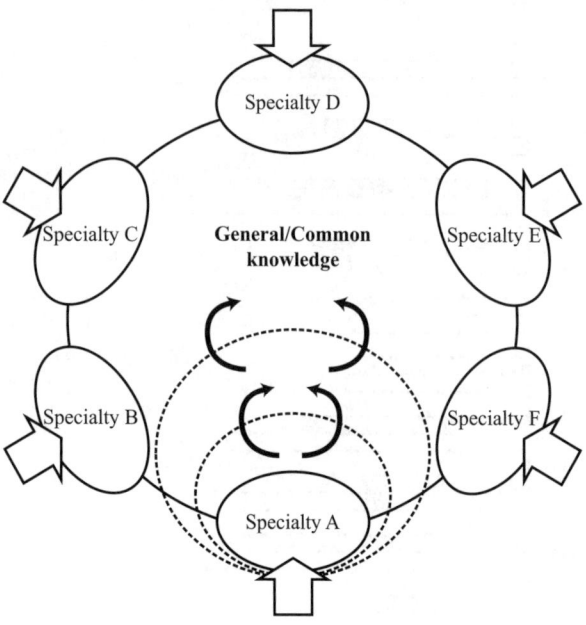

vocational relevance of educational curricula should be designed to contain ample flexibility, at the same time maintaining the outlines of each specialized field. The concept 'flexpeciality' is useful for depicting the necessary competence to be achieved through education (Figure 6.7).

Second, the convention of periodically blanket recruiting new graduates should be opened to those who continue job seeking and those who become non-regular workers after graduation. The opportunity to become a regular worker should be open to everyone who has the appropriate competence, experience, and volition. The current situation, where those who failed to get a regular job upon graduation are disadvantaged for life, needs to be resolved.

Third, the wage gap between regular and non-regular workers needs to be narrowed. The pay for non-regular workers should be based on the principle of 'equal pay for equal work' so that they can attain an acceptable standard of living. I propose that a transitional labor market, which bridges regular and non-regular workers, should be established; this would include, for instance, regular employment with shorter working hours and non-regular employment with more stable working conditions and an upward career path.

Fourth, greater opportunities for vocational training outside of companies should be created. This is required, at least in part, because budgets for vocational training within companies are currently in decline. Even regular workers are no longer guaranteed opportunities to improve their skill levels. For non-regular workers, there are even fewer opportunities for improving occupational skills. Therefore, many more inexpensive public training opportunities, which are very limited in Japan at present, should be provided outside of companies, preferably with trainees' living expenses for the unemployed and precarious workers.

Finally, vocational guidance and counseling should be available to a wider range of young people. To date, vocational guidance has been limited to students at school. However, with increasing numbers of non-regular workers and jobless youth, opportunities for vocational guidance and counseling should be made available to graduates as well. Youth support institutions, which provide various kinds of help and information as one-stop services, need to be increased. Labor unions are also expected to play a role in supporting and empowering young workers regardless of working styles.

Figure 6.8 is a model envisaged for the Japanese youth labor market. In order to tackle the problems of 'dualism' within the labor

Figure 6.8: Envisaged model of youth labor market

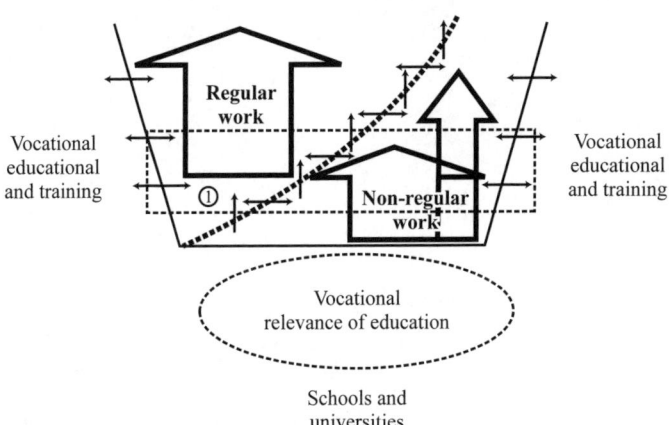

① Youth support institutions and labour unions

market, this model seems to be the only credible solution. Needless to say, reforming the labor market is no easy task, but that fact itself adds urgency to determined efforts. To leave the situation unattended will inflict major damage on the well-being of individuals and on the sustainability of Japanese society.

7 Policies against Social Exclusion in France

Xavier Emmanuelli

After defining the notion of exclusion and assessing its scope, we shall review the experience of the generous public policies which have been set up in France regarding the establishment of social minima and making certain fundamental rights efficient, such as the right to housing. We shall see finally that modes of action are being reshaped and that this might provide best efficiency, for instance, with respect to shelterless populations.

Definition and scope of the notion of exclusion

Exclusion, a phenomenon with multiple implications

The notion of exclusion may be confusing: the homeless, disabled, long-term unemployed, poorly housed, and Minimum Insertion Income beneficiaries may be gathered under the same designation.

A central idea, put forward by French experts and relayed Europewide, is to see exclusion as an accumulation of disabilities, beyond the simple monetary aspects of poverty: the non-participation in productive life (in particular through work), the absence of consumption, the absence of (political, associative, etc) commitment and the absence of social interactions are the main characteristics of an "excluded" person.

The notion of social exclusion hence reflects the non-realization of certain rights for members of society. It gives birth to the opposite notion of insertion. Thus, policies against exclusion encompass a collection of interventions and social rights, whose principal aims are the insertion of unfavored people and the access to rights.

Alongside the homeless, who represent the ultimate stage of social exclusion, poor workers are another contemporary figure of exclusion It can be reliably estimated that the number of poor workers (those earning 50% or less of the median income) has remained steady at around 1.3 or 1.4 million since 2000.

Progressive institutionalization of the policies against exclusions

With increasing unemployment, and especially long-term unemployment, in France since the beginning of the 1980s, the notion of exclusion designates a new type of poverty that the social policies implemented after the Second World War have failed to curb.

The social protection system set up in 1945 is based upon the insurance cover of the wage-earner and his assignees. Alongside this system, social help, which is funded by the national solidarity and hence the state, addresses quite targeted categories of people (disabled, families with children, etc).

Founded on professional bases, the social security system is undermined by unemployment, to the extent that those who benefited from it before as well as those who might benefit from it should they still hold a stable job, are now precluded from its services. In this sense, the "excluded" are excluded from the mechanisms of the Social Security System and from the major project of social democracy.

The insertion policies which were institutionalized in the 1980s include two main aspects: fighting against poverty and access to employment. The fight against poverty, still associated with the services provided by the former welfare policies, also seeks to guarantee people's dignity and the protection of their rights. The fight against exclusion has two structuring features: access to rights and to insertion. Assisted people are no longer considered as social misfits or outcasts, but as citizens with economic, civic and social rights which ought to be asserted.

If one considers that the whole social protection system contributes to fighting against exclusion, 526 billion Euros (30 percent of GDP) were allocated to the fight against exclusion. From an accounting perspective, the fight against exclusion is but one element among the social protection services offered. All this "poverty and social exclusion" risk is associated with the Minimum Insertion Income, with expenses in 2006 amounting to 8 billion Euros, or a mere 1.5 percent of the total social protection services offered.

As regards social accounts *stricto sensu*, the fight against exclusion seems to be marginal (1.6 percent in 2004, see Figure 7.1). It still goes without saying that a portion of each of the other risks

Figure 7.1: Risk-related apportionment of social protection services offered (2004)

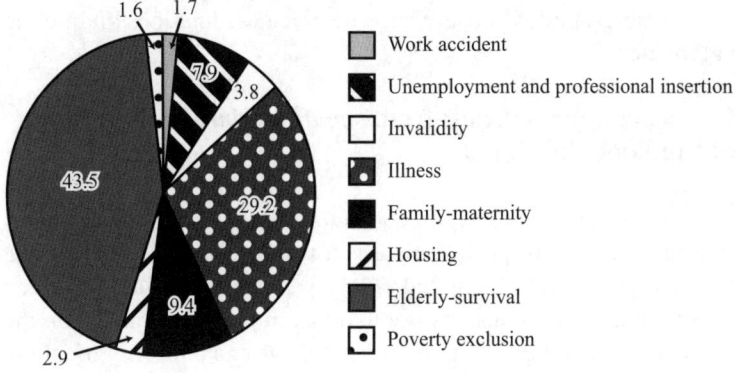

Source: Direction de la recherche, des études, de l'évaluation et des statistiques (DREES), *Comptes de la protection sociale*, 2004

can be seen as associated, at least implicitly, with objectives to fight against exclusion. We could also mention family services, housing aids or unemployment insurance that are not taken into account.

Multiple actors

The state, as the safe-keeper of national solidarity, runs and co-ordinates policies against major social exclusions; as such, it is the first responsible for assisting the shelterless. The primacy of the state's intervention with respect to the territorial collectivities, in particular, can be justified by a specific duty of the state in favor of persons who cannot be attached to a local territory.

This continuous movement of the state, where it was the only actor in fighting against all kinds of exclusions, was interrupted in 2003 when a new step of decentralization transferred the management of Minimum Insertion Income and the general responsibility for social help to departments. The department has become the single leader in social policies, while the state keeps a major role in sharing responsibilities.

The associative sector is an essential actor of the policies against exclusion. The state is engaged in a growing process of delegation to associations, entrusting them with the management of public housing services. Said associations operate national and local policies against exclusion; they benefit from financial support which often represents their whole budget. We are therefore talking about mutual dependence between associations and public authorities.

General public policies: from *social minima* to the efficacy of fundamental rights

Fighting exclusion has become a major objective of public policies in France. In this respect, Article 1 of the Orientation Law Relative to the Fight against Excluded (29 July 1998) is particularly clear. "The fight against exclusions is a national imperative founded on the respect of equal dignity of all human beings and a priority of all the public policies of the nation."

The interventions and policies conducted on behalf of the fight against exclusion no longer aim solely to preserve society against the feared collective consequences of poverty, but the efficacy of the fundamental rights of individuals confronted with the various consequences of poverty.

Social minima

The social minima are social aid and action in favor of unfavored people in the form of national legal services providing a minimum of resources. The French system entails nine social minima: the expression denotes benefits which bring a person's or a household's resources up to a minimum level. Their amount is calculated as the difference between the beneficiary's resources and the resource ceiling, limited to the maximum amount of the benefit. In 2006, 18 billion Euros were dedicated to social minima.

At the end of 2006, 3.5 million people were beneficiaries of at least one of these services. When including assignees (recipients' partners and children), more than 6 million people were covered by the social minima, that is, 10 percent of the French population. Some of the social minima are family-based, inasmuch as their amount takes into account the size of the household. Other social minima are individual-based.

The different social minima are as follows:
- the disability minimum benefit

- the insertion benefit (AI)
- the specific solidarity benefit (ASS)
- the minimum old-age income
- the disabled adult allowance (AAH)
- the widowhood insurance allowance
- the single-parent allowance (API)
- the pension equivalent allowance (AER)

The most known is indisputably the Minimum Insertion Income (RMI), which covers 1.3 million people. The RMI is a department-financed allowance whose aim is to help people in distress recover social and financial autonomy. The payment of that allowance is subject to signing an insertion agreement with the department.

Nonetheless, the policy against exclusion does not solely amount to allocating a minimum income; its purpose is also to secure certain rights.

Social housing policy

For the state, the right to housing remains one of the vectors of social cohesion and of the fight against exclusions. The 31 May 1990 Act consecrates the right to housing and sets forth that "securing the right to housing constitutes a duty of solidarity for the whole nation". It involves two tools: the departmental action plan in favor of housing for vulnerable households (PDLPD) and the solidarity fund for housing (FSL), to oppose a last rampart against housing exclusion.

The 5 March 2007 Act sets forth a justiciable right to housing which creates an obligation of result from the state (to find a roof for the homeless).[1] This justiciable right to housing is provided for all those who cannot obtain social housing within "reasonable" timeframes as of January 2012 but in the meantime, it will be reserved to "priority" households already amounting to more than 600,000 people and regarding the homeless, families housed in hotel-type accommodation, tenants threatened with expulsion without re-housing, households living in unsafe buildings, etc.

The state provides the conditions under which the construction of "social housing" and of "very social housing" is financed for accommodating fragilized populations by building moderate rental homes through government-subsidized loans. On 1 January 2003, one main residence in six was social housing. The "Solidarity and urban renewal" law, which came into force in 2000, compels towns to offer at least 20% social housing.

Finally, the state distributes housing aids to low-income tenants It also addresses targeted populations, for instance young people, for securing access to housing to all.

Town policy

Created some thirty years ago, the town policy is the urban aspect of the policies against exclusion. The town policy includes all the actions to fight against the exclusion of unfavored urban populations. It is first of all a contractual policy, a global policy encompassing all aspects of daily life, and an inter-ministerial policy.

Its field of application covers six major fields:
- urban redevelopment
- safety
- delinquency prevention
- social and cultural development of the districts
- development of employment
- economic revitalization of these districts.

Over recent years, new orientations have been assigned to the town policy, with new tools focused on urban redevelopment, i.e. the radical transformation of these territories, via demolition and reconstruction of buildings.

Economy-based insertion

Economy-based insertion is twofold. First, the "state-aided contracts" which in the merchant and non-merchant sectors seek to maintain (or bring back) on the labor market people cut-off from employment (hiring incentives allocated to the employer as well as training and qualification opportunities offered to most of them).

Second, a collection of companies and associations (insertion companies, intermediate associations, insertion schemes) which benefit from public aid and support for the supervision and follow-up of employees with weakened productive capacities, but recruited in order to benefit from a wage-earning activity (subsidies, direct aid to workplaces or exemptions from social contributions). In 2005, "IAE" aid represented close to 150 million Euros. At the end of 2005, 500,000 people benefited from a state-aided contract, for an annual public expense of approximately 6 billion Euros.

Unfavored people's health

Unfavored people's health is a concern which has materialized in laws. In this view, the 27 July 1999 Act, regarding universal health cover (CMU) creates a right to have health insurance expenses reimbursed and intends to secure access to care. At the beginning of 2007, close to 5 million people were covered by complementary universal health cover mechanism and 1.5 million only by the basic universal health cover.

Public homeless assistance policy

The homeless is the most visible figure of exclusion. According to the National Institute of Statistics and Economic Studies, the homeless can be defined as people who, on any occasion, had to spend the night in a location which is not intended for habitation as well as those supported by an organization providing housing free of charge or for a small contribution. In this context, the Institute estimates that 90,000 people are homeless.

The investigation conducted by the National Institute of Statistics and Economic Studies in 2001 highlights a few features: the homeless are mostly young men, including four times more foreigners than in the general population, a high proportion of young adults aged between 18 and 29, as well as a significant presence of young women and of people with one or several children. Close to one-third of the homeless have jobs.

A convoluted and complex assistance system

Until the 1970s, the shelterless had been assisted by the associations. Since the 1980s, actions regarding the homeless have gradually been institutionalized and public policies for the benefit of shelterless people have emerged little by little. Under the pressure of the needs, numerous devices have been designed for assisting the people sleeping rough until a specific assistance system has been developed for the homeless. The French case stands out from the other European cases: high centralization, sizeable means, wide offering, far-reaching consensus and low criminalization.

In 1993, we created the Homeless Rescue Service in Paris with the first Mobile Help Teams whose mission consists in "walking out to meet the people who, on the streets, appear to be in physical or social distress" for providing assistance or making contact with them. Such is the principle of cruising around the streets.

Consequently, the emergency accommodation scheme rests on two types of tools: the teams in charge of the social watch and the accommodation centers properly speaking.

The social watch, which directs assisted populations towards accommodation solutions, is ensured by four entities:
- dialing 115, an emergency telephone service available in every French Department
- reception and orientation services (SAO)
- mobile teams of the homeless rescue service cruising around the streets
- day assistance centers.

Emergency accommodation places are situated in emergency shelters (CHUs) or in structures, such as the Accommodation and Social Rehabilitation Centers (CHRS), which keep a number of places available to that end. The specificity of these places is the short duration of the stay allowed. Furthermore, since 1991, the assistance to temporary housing (ALT) enables the development of emergency accommodation capacities.

This has added a few thousand adapted housing places: social residences and boarding houses. In April 2007, the French Accounts Court, dedicated to homeless people, reports 24,000 emergency places and more than 180,000 places in social mediation housing and temporary housing.

In parallel, since 1984, winter specific measures have been taken every year. In addition to the prohibition of expulsions, the winter scheme includes the possibility for the Préfets to increase the number of emergency accommodation places by requisitioning gymnasiums, army barracks or metro stations. The mobile teams are also likely to cruise the streets more intensively.

The year 2007 was a watershed year for emergency accommodation since in-depth transformations were brought about by: the implementation of the Reinforced Action Plan for shelterless people (PARSA); the institution of a justiciable right to housing (DALO) by the 25 March 2007 Act strengthening the principle of continuity for assisting shelterless people. This right enables any shelterless person to lodge a complaint against the state, when there is no housing provided to said person.

Towards reshuffled modes of action and more efficient public policies

Reshuffled public modes of action

The assessment of public policies has highlighted obstacles that prevent the schemes set up to fight against exclusion from proving truly fruitful. The absence of legibility of the schemes (for the recipients as well as for the go-betweens), the dilution of responsibilities, the primacy of management over efficiency, the geographical disparities, and the poor diffusion of information ought to be noted. Thus, over the past few years, several inflections in the public modes of action can be observed:

The increased recourse to "partnership" (alongside the parity aims of the Social security system): The notion of partnership is central to reshuffling public cooperation and decision-making modes. The "partnership" hence appears as a modality of joint action. Actors, fitted with variable powers, join forces and throw in ideas so as to make decisions and conduct a project together. However, the partnership may drift towards bureaucratization and undecidability.

The growing position of the associative sector: The associative sector is an essential actor of policies against exclusion. The state is engaged in a process of increasing delegation to the associations, entrusting them with the principal management of public hosting services. Said associations operate national and local policies against exclusion, and benefit from financial support which often represents their entire budget. At the end of the day, associations and public authorities form a negotiated, contractualized and nested system which is based upon recognizing the professionalism of the associations and on public financing schemes.

The strongly asserted concern for territories and local particularities: The aim of the recent laws is to clarify control at the local level and delineate the actions to be implemented by local actors. The idea is to set quantitative objectives based upon increased effort for evaluating needs.

Simplified and more efficient devices

An overview of the insertion policies has highlighted three complications: increasingly complex social mediation devices; too small gains when retrieving a job; the amplification of the poor workers' phenomenon. In light of these observations, the state has turned to structural reforms via reforms of the social minima for combining work-based incomes and transfer incomes by creating the Active Solidarity Income (*Revenu de solidarité active:* RSA) which is substituted for the Minimum Insertion Income (RMI).

The Active Solidarity Income (RSA): reforming the social minima to provide "an active solidarity"
The reform of the social minima builds upon the observation that the purpose of social protection is not only to compensate for and remedy the absence of work, but to prepare and accompany the activity in the interest of all. The general objective of the reforms to the social minima is to: improve incentives to work and the outputs of welfare programs, simplify social aid, provide a monetary contribution to people whose incomes are too low to leave poverty behind and create more favorable conditions when employing said people.

The Active Solidarity Income (RSA) came into force on 1 June 2009 and guarantees a minimum income whose amount varies according to household composition and to the household's activity-based income. This RSA is calculated by an evaluation of a minimum income as the sum of 62% of the household's activity-based incomes plus the regulatory amount corresponding to the household composition, then an allowance is calculated, as the difference between this minimum income and the total amount perceived by the household: its activity-based income and possibly a housing allowance. This will complement the resources of the household. It comprises recognition of the rights and duties of the recipients and priority is given to guidance towards employment.

It intends to ensure that any return to work, however minimal, increases the effectively available income, which should avoid threshold effects and the all too often associated inactivity traps. Furthermore, to make the offering of state-aided contracts more legible, the law created, as of January 2010, a single insertion contract building upon two modalities, one in the merchant sector and the other one in the non-merchant sector.

Towards the modernization of the homeless assistance system

A partnership approach has been developed between the state and the associations this year and has led to the observation that the assistance system as implemented in the 1990s must be rethought. A

roadmap based on reshaping the accommodation policy for shelterless people has thus been adopted around 5 objectives:
1. setting up observation, information and results assessment systems
2. simplifying the accommodation offering system, including the construction of a reference range of services to obtain a simpler and more legible architecture of the scheme
3. reforming the way houseless people are supported (rationalization and mutualization of emergency means) and building gradual and individual-based courses, whereas the idea is to allocate a single social worker to the persons assisted;
4. adopting a territorial and multi-year planning approach of offerings similar to that provided in the healthcare system;
5. ensuring the accommodation scheme which prioritizes access to housing, whether ordinary or adapted.

To conclude, policies against social exclusion continue to require improvement. It should be noted that judicious reform paths must involve substantial objectives to be set for fighting against poverty (for instance setting ambitious goals such as "zero poor children within 15 years" or "zero homeless within 5 years").

8 Public Policies toward Homeless and the Politicization of Civil Society in Japan

David-Antoine Malinas

Introduction

In the early 1990s homelessness became a new urban and social problem in Japan. Homelessness first began to be visible on the streets of Tokyo and Osaka and then in other large and middle range cities. All local authorities began to take measures to cope with this new phenomenon. Tokyo, however, stands out. In the capital, the measures taken were both radical and versatile. This was especially the case in the measures taken toward the homeless living in Shinjuku ward, where the third largest homeless community in Tokyo had settled in the underground streets of Shinjuku station. The Tokyo Metropolitan Government (TMG) evicted them twice, first in February 1994 and then in January 1996. These were the largest evictions ever in Japan.

At the beginning of 1998, however, TMG adopted a different approach to this community. They were to experience the TMG's first social policy specifically targeting homelessness, which was eventually implemented in all Tokyo wards from 2000. The program inspired other major cities, such as Osaka, to adopt more socially oriented policies. In short, this local policy change had a strong impact not only on the homeless people in Shinjuku but more broadly on homeless policies all around Japan. In this chapter, my aim is to explain the rise and fall of policies toward homeless people: how can we explain TMG's shift from a repressive to an inclusive social policy? To answer this question we need to examine the decision processes that led to both the repressive policy and to the inclusive policy.

Policy making processes entail the interaction of many actors. In the case of policies for poor people, the first actors to be taken into consideration are the local authorities that implement the policies. To understand the changes in policy direction from this variable would be difficult, however, because the same governor with a strong prejudice toward homeless people governed Tokyo during the entire period being considered. Second we must consider the homeless themselves. As is often the case for poor and stigmatized populations, they do not have enough power or influence to modify or initiate policies. The change of policies from repressive to inclusive is not directly attributable to their actions. My hypothesis is that special attention must be given to a third actor: civil society. This actor strongly determined the evolution of policies toward the homeless. Interest in civil society in Japan is not very strong, but became stronger after the passage of the 1998 NPO law. However, most studies in this field focus on 'independent' civil society, working as a substitute for, or with little or no influence on, the authorities (Pekkanen 2006; Avenell 2009). There are few studies that have focused on political activism in civil society except to point out that it is in decline, describing the decay of environmental activism or the fragmentation of the peace movement. These accounts are accurate but they overlook a new dynamic. My argument is that poverty and inequality have revitalized the political dimension of civil society, starting in the 1990s.

The change of policy direction regarding the homeless in Shinjuku illustrates in detail the early stage of this politicization process. I distinguish two types of activism that have influenced Tokyo's policies. I call the first one 'parochial activism': the activism of local inhabitants who defend the quality of life of their local community and see homeless people as a neighborhood nuisance, advocating for their eviction. This activism was very strong in the early 1990s, and was one of the major factors in the double eviction of the homeless from Shinjuku in 1994 and 1996. Confronting this NIMBY (Not in My Back Yard) activism are the advocates of homeless people's rights. The latter group grew stronger after the first eviction in Shinjuku, organizing homeless people into the first organization called the coalition of Shinjuku (In Japanese *Shinjuku Renraku Kai*), and struggling for four years to obtain a change in policy.

Repressive policies toward homeless people

We will first focus on parochial activism and its influence on the politics of exclusion regarding homeless people. Although local activism has not always been political, the history of its political mobilization shows a strong commitment to defend the rights of minorities. This is a common characteristic of a wide array of local protest actions, ranging from opposition to the construction of Narita international airport to the opposition to various dam projects. A nuclear plant might bring a benefit for many citizens in the form of electricity but a minority would have to bear the danger of living in its vicinity. In certain cases, both local and national interests aggregate. Such is the case of Minamata, where the pollution of the local community by corporate negligence eventually highlighted the hidden costs of economic growth and brought about new environmental standards. However, when the homeless problem arose in the early 1990s, parochial activism showed a new face. Although local communities often defended the interests of the few—that is, their own interests—they were not eager to take into consideration the interests of the even fewer. Because homeless people were not considered to be members of the community, their presence in local public space was considered to be an environmental problem, or an 'urban problem' that should be dealt with. In the most extreme cases, such as in Shinjuku, local activism triggered strong containment and eviction policies by local authorities.

The first action of parochial activism was to contain access to the welfare support called *seikatsu hogo* (Life Protection). In Japan, the welfare minimum is financed both by the central state and the local authorities. If a local welfare office were to allow homeless people access to welfare support, it would constitute a burden on the local budget. And if only one welfare office out of the 23 wards in Tokyo provided support to homeless people, the homeless people of Tokyo would concentrate in this very ward, creating a strong demand on the welfare budget and rapidly increasing the burden. Residents of the ward, and local tax-payers, would then criticize the misuse of tax revenue to support people who do not pay local taxes and are seen as 'free riders'. This was the criticism directed at the director of the welfare office in Shinjuku when it provided some ad-hoc welfare support services during 1994. During an interview in 2003 he said:

> Until the early 1990s, homeless were people who used to live in Shinjuku ward and to pay taxes. So, the inhabitants of the ward accepted that their taxes were used to help these people. But when the number of homeless people rose and the newcomers had no prior connection to Shinjuku, Shinjuku ward inhabitants became much more reluctant about using their taxes to help people they did not know.

That is the reason why during the town-hall meetings I had to face numerous critics. I have been asked: 'Why should citizens of Shinjuku have to pay for people who have never contributed to Shinjuku's community?' I have to acknowledge that it was an uncomfortable situation for me. (Interview, Takeyama san, April 2003)

Consequently, different actions were taken by the welfare office to limit access to Life Protection. The first action was to refuse access to Life Protection application form. One inappropriate technique used to justify this was to require people to prove that they have a registered address in the ward. This was a response to the demand to ensure that local tax payer money was only spent to help people who lived and paid taxes locally. By law, there is no requirement that one be a member of the local community to obtain Life Protection benefits, but with this restriction the welfare office achieved two goals. First, it assured the local tax-payers and voters that taxes were used only to sustain people of the local community. Second, and more obviously, it denied access for almost all homeless people, whether local or not, because none of them had an address—they were living on the street.

In some cases, demands for the application documents could not be denied. However, there are other ways to limit the number of homeless who receive welfare support. One is to subject applicants to a medical examination, in which a doctor can determine whether they are physically fit for work or not. This practice raises two immediate concerns. First, as pointed out by Kitagawa (2005), is that in such an examination, the capacity to work is assessed solely on the physical condition of the individual; there is no consideration of the situation in the job market. That is, the fact that a person is physically able to work does not necessarily mean that they can actually find a job. Nevertheless, they can be denied welfare support on this basis, even though they have few chances of finding a job. Second is the implementation of an intermediary diagnostic, 'fit for light duties', which is often used when the person is not severely physically disabled. With this 'fitness' criteria, despite the growing number of people on the street during the 1990s, the number of people who receive the social welfare payment remains more or less stable during the period.

The second policy that was supported by parochial activism was eviction. In Shinjuku, the involvement of inhabitants in the eviction policy has a long history. In 1980 the commerce association joined a group created by the Shinjuku Town Hall called the 'Committee for the Purification of the Shinjuku Station Surroundings' (*Shinjuku eki shūhen kankyō jōka taisaku kaigi*). The official aim of this committee was to fight against homeless, 'barkers, drug addicts, homosexuals, illegal garbage disposal, ticket scalpers, illegally parked bicycles and noise' (Shinjuku Ward Information Newsletter, 15 November, 1983 cited in Hasegawa 2006). Though the list is long, the main focus of the committee would be to exclude the homeless from this public space. During its first years, the committee patrolled the area on a weekly base, asking the homeless not to sleep in the underground of Shinjuku station. Then the pace intensified such that in 1982–1983, for example, members of the patrol made about 4000 requests to homeless people to leave the area (Shinjuku Ward Newsletter, November 15, 1983). However, this eviction policy had limited results and became increasingly ineffective as growing numbers of homeless people began to settle in this public space in the early 1990s. The committee stopped its patrol activities in 1994, but the eviction policies remain in place.

TMG, whose offices were relocated in Shinjuku in 1991, adopted an eviction policy named: "Eviction of Materials that Uncomb Public Space" (*rojō haizai tekkyo sagyō*), which focused on the removal of homeless people's cardboard houses. However the results were very limited and the number of homeless people settling in Shinjuku continued to grow. Also, TMG decided to proceed with two large-scale evictions, the first in 1994 and the second in 1996. The decision to implement more repressive policies was a response to the complaints of the local shop owners' association, which was concerned that commerce in the underground would suffer from the presence of homeless settlements. But this decision was also supported by the governor, who had a strong prejudice against homeless people. He declared his view during a press conference that:

> These people, they have a particular way to understand life, a specific philosophy. Even if you offer them a job or dwelling, they will refuse... [B]ut they should understand that they are a nuisance on the street, they should feel guiltier than they are. (20 October 1995)

As it was an official press conference, he was not expressing the view as a private citizen but as an officially elected representative of millions. He was not alone in his view.

The vast majority of Japanese perceived homeless people in negative terms. A very rare multiple choice opinion poll of perceptions of homeless people reveals a very high concentration of negative terms (Morita 2001). If we eliminate the answer 'lonely' (41%), the top four answers are 'unhealthy' (67.6%), 'dirty' (67.5%), 'lazy' (51%), and 'scary' (33.6%). The answer 'pitiful' (21.2%) and 'suffering' (15.8%) did not enter the top ten. Moreover, homelessness was typically seen as a conscious life-style decision. In the early 1990s, the common myth, part of the post-second world war policy heritage, that everybody could find a job if he was 'truly' looking for it, remained very strong. Hence, homelessness was rarely considered to be a consequence of a deteriorating job market or welfare system, but was rather viewed from a moral perspective as people who would choose to no longer assume their responsibilities—as a worker, a husband and father—in 'normal' society. This collective understanding of homelessness shaped homeless policies for many years despite the efforts of various officials to point out its limits. As the director of the welfare office of Shinjuku ward observed:

> There were demands for evicting the homeless, especially coming from the shop owners. But if we evict them, what happens? They just move in another public location, another park for instance. Then, because other inhabitants cannot use it, one more time, there will be a demand for eviction, and we would have to evict them again. It was not the answer, especially during this period when the homeless demographic was on the rise. (Interview, Takeyama san, April 2003)

In Shinjuku, the parochial mobilization against homeless people has been strong. Even when the local authorities' policy became more inclusive, shop owners would hire private guards to patrol the underground and evict homeless people. This attitude is far from exceptional. There are regular reports in the press of homeless people being attacked—beaten or killed—by 'normal' people. There are also regular instances of verbal aggression or 'light' assaults such as tossing a lit cigarette butt onto a sleeping homeless person. Although they are not reported in the media, the homeless report these incidences when they are questioned about them. Today, as Japan is dealing with the consequences of the global financial crisis, homelessness is increasingly understood to be a consequence of the deteriorating economy and less as a personal choice. This 'new' understanding of the situation has been promoted by homeless' advocates since the beginning of the 1990s. It was first raised as a challenge to TMG's repressive policy against the homeless people of Shinjuku and gave birth to the first inclusive policy.

Inclusive policy toward homeless people

I will now focus on the activism of the supporters of homeless' rights. One of the first organizations of this type was founded in Shinjuku. It was named the *Shinjuku Renraku Kai* (SRK) or 'Coalition of Shinjuku'. Besides homeless people, it included members of two radical left groups who, for the first time, joined forces in the same organizational structure. One of these groups was the 'Sogidan', a day laborers' union founded in the early 1980s, whose activity was primarily located in North East Tokyo in a day-laborer ghetto called Sanya. Most of the members had prior experience as student activists. They were members of the students' political groups called *sekuto*, or 'sects', which led the student revolution in the 1970s. Their ideological reference was Revolutionary Marxism or Maoism. The other group was named 'Inoken', a combination of two words meaning 'life' (*inochi*) and 'right' (*kenri*). Its members supported foreign workers who had lost their jobs, and hence their working visas, when the recession began in the early 1990s. Without visas, they became illegal immigrants, and were deported by the migration police. Inoken members opposed this policy with no success. The majority of its members were students who were affiliated with the 'non-sect' student groups. It was created in the 1970s in a reaction against the violence of the other 'sects'. The common ideology of its members was Anarchism. Because most of these radical left groups were using violence as a mean for social change, as well as for internal bloody purges, they would not generally be considered to be desirable agents of change in the Japanese democratic system (Hasegawa and Machimura 2004). When considering the TMG homeless policy, however, we must acknowledge the influence of the radical left groups that composed the SRK. I therefore analyze the influence of these activists on the TMG's homeless policy, both as agents of resistance and change.

After the 1994 eviction, these activists mobilized homeless people to resist further repressive policies by the TMG. This mobilization was successful in several ways. First, it delayed the second general eviction by several weeks. Although it was supposed to take place at the end of 1995, it did not take place until January 1996. During this moratorium period the SRK initiated numerous actions and received constant media coverage by national newspapers such as Mainichi, Asahi and Yomiuri. Below is a list of the main actions that were reported in the press in December 1995 and January 1996:

- 8 December: TMG eviction plan is officially presented; SRK protests against the plan
- 11 December: SRK demonstration
- 14 December: SRK demonstration
- 13 January: Opposition to the TMG's distribution of flyers to inform homeless people of the reasons for their coming eviction. Three militants arrested
- 19 January: SRK asks the Japanese Bar Association for support to have the evictions declared to be illegal
- 23 January: SRK demands compromise

Although it is more difficult to retrieve television archives and the reports of other local media, intense press coverage indicates that the eviction of the homeless people of Shinjuku on 23 January became one of the first major events of 1996. Also, for the first time the general public's opinion was supportive of the homeless and critical of the TMG eviction policy. When the eviction was carried out on 23 January, many articles condemning the TMG's action were published. Furthermore, the TMG was inundated with critical messages delivered directly via a new service called 'Proposition to the Governor' (*chiji he no teigen*). About 1400 messages were received by mail and fax, most of them opposed to the eviction policy. This represents almost one-quarter of the messages that were sent to 'Proposition to the Governor' in fiscal year 1995 (April 1995—March 1996) and makes the eviction policy the most commented action of the TMG.

Another important point is that homeless people remained in the underground. Although they were evicted on 23 January from their location on one of the underground streets, they re-settled almost immediately on an adjacent underground street with the SRK's support. The poor results of the TMG action was condemned by local shop owners who had been hoping to be rid of the homeless people. The governor, who was elected on a promise to use tax payer's money more responsibly, was also subjected to harsh criticism for the failures of this policy. After the SRK successfully lobbied the TMG's financial collaborators—the Japan Lottery Association and Shinjuku Ward—to withdraw from the project, the TMG had to bear the total financial cost of the eviction, including the cost of the re-zoning and the construction of a giant underground moving sidewalk. With a total cost of more than 1.64 billion yen (approx $10 million) for a result close to none, TMG lost the support of both the tax-payers and the parochially mobilized groups that had been agitating for the eviction of the homeless. The parochial groups did not, however, give up on evicting the homeless from the underground. After the failure of the January 24th eviction, private patrols reportedly began to patrol the underground of Shinjuku asking homeless people to leave. It appears that it was the local shop owners who decided to employ them (Interview with Inaba san,[1] May 2005; Hasegawa 2006). The failure of the 1996 eviction produced a rift between the TMG and the parochial mobilizations, which became even more pronounced as the TMG decided to abandon the eviction policy and develop an insertion policy.

For TMG, the reinsertion shelter that was established in conjunction with the eviction policy of 1996 provided strong evidence of a different way to cope with the homeless problem. As mentioned, homeless people were widely believed to have chosen their street life, but the data coming from the shelter painted a very different picture. Although few homeless joined the program—only about 70 people in a 300 person capacity shelter—about 75% percent of them found jobs. This indicated that if homeless people were given support, there would be fewer of them on the street, which of course had significant political benefits. Hence, from 1996, TMG began to develop a new policy, but its top-down attempt at rapid implementation faced multiple points of resistance. In fiscal year 1997, opposition rose from the wards. To implement a city-wide homeless policy, all 23 wards had to cooperate financially, and some of them had to accept the construction of shelters in their local areas. It took many years to achieve a consensus between the 23 wards and TMG. Thus, in fiscal year 1998, as negotiations were going on, TMG decided to run a solo pilot project in Shinjuku. But it immediately encountered another source of resistance: residents did not want a homeless shelter constructed near their homes. TMG was confronted with yet another 'parochial mobilization' challenging its new policy. Rather surprisingly, it was the homeless advocates from the SRK who would trigger this latest outbreak of NIMBYism. And, rather confusingly, this indicates that there was a coalition of interests between the local residents and the advocates for the homeless. Why did the SRK oppose the TMG policy?

There were three mains reasons, two of which were internal to the advocacy group. When confronted with the eviction policy, all of the militants rallied in opposition. In a sense, the TMG's repressive policy bound together people with different ideas. However, when it comes to implementing inclusive policies, the members of the Sogidan and the Inoken had quite different positions on what should be done. The members of the Sogidan defended an employment policy, as might be expected of a day-laborers' union. They had supported day laborers for many years, but as these workers aged, they could not find jobs anymore. Furthermore, the principal objective of the union had always been to pressure local authorities to provide jobs for unemployed day laborers who lived on the streets. As can be seen in the archives of the SRK, the first demand of the SRK—reflecting the view of the members of the Sogidan—was related to job provision:

I An employment policy for day labor workers living on the street of Shinjuku
  1 That Shinjuku ward, following the August 15 (1995) demand of the economic and employment office of Tokyo Metropolitan Government offers day-labor workers who live in Shinjuku (including homeless) a guaranteed job...
  2 That Shinjuku ward, toward workers who are more and more numerous on the street, and in the limit of its administrative competence, create immediately an employment policy for the workers who are on the streets of Shinjuku.
                                             (Shinjuku Renraku Kai 1995: 20)

Moreover, it should be noted that the members of Sogidan would not refer to homeless people as 'homeless' but used the term 'unemployed day laborers'. Until the early 1990s, the majority of homeless people in Japanese cities were from the day-labor ghetto. As Inaba recalls:

In 1994, the homeless would not let us call them homeless. One day, we asked a group of about 50 people how they would like us to call them. The most frequent answer was day-laborers, because most of them were day-laborers who had lost their jobs. (Interview, Inaba san, November 2002)

Neither the SRK nor the homeless themselves had demanded the provision of shelters; as most of them being day-labor workers, few had experience of permanent dwellings. They were accustomed to sleeping in cheap hotels or in barracks within the construction site. In the warm days of summer, because the small rooms would be too hot, some of them would prefer to sleep outside (*aozora*). Hence, a policy that would prioritize a dwelling place before a job did not meet the demands of either the homeless or their advocates.

The Inoken members' position was different. They rejected the shelter policy, and any inclusive policy, in defense of the homeless people's right to live on the street as an alternative way of life. For the members of Inoken, the problem of homeless people and that of migrant people (their original cause) are the same: the fact that authorities do not recognize cultural diversity and act to extinguish it. As Inaba explained:

> The eviction of Iranian workers in 1993 and then the eviction of homeless people in 1994. In both cases, people were treated as things. When you need them you use them. When it is a crisis and you don't need them anymore, you throw them away. That is the reason why with other members of the Inoken group we moved up to Shinjuku. (Interview, Inaba san, November 2002)

Members of the Inoken promoted a stable life on the street, and aimed to strengthen 'community empowerment'. For instance, Inaba claimed that examples of community empowerment were very common in Asia: 'There are many of them in India or in China. They are ghettos inside which people work together to improve their life conditions and struggle against authorities' eviction policies' (Interview, Inaba san, November 2002). Thus, for different ideological reasons, advocates for the homeless were reluctant to support the TMG's shelter policy.

The SRK's resistance to the TMG's policy was not driven only by ideological reasons, however. There was also a strategic dimension to their refusal. When TMG was developing its insertion policy for the homeless, it refused to have the SRK involved in the negotiations. And after the second eviction of 1996, TMG tried to destroy the SRK by putting two of its leaders on trial. Although this action weakened the movement temporarily, the TMG dropped the charges—obstruction against public officers—after a few months and the leaders came back. When the TMG tried in fiscal years 1996 and 1997 to implement an inclusive policy, it did not consult with the SRK. Also, as we have seen, the SRK refused to support the TMG's shelter policy. Moreover, when the SRK learned that TMG was about to construct a shelter for homeless people in Shinjuku, they associated with the local residents to resist the proposal. Thus, from 1996 to 1998, parochial mobilization and homeless advocates opposed the TMG's inclusive policy. Although their reasons differed, they shared certain objectives and found that it was in their mutual interest to cooperate. Lacking the support of both the civil society and the wards, TMG could not implement its homeless policy.

This confusing situation evolved in early 1998. For two years, TMG had not evicted any homeless, and inside the SRK, the ideological reasons for rejecting the shelter policy were weakening. Especially in the second half of the 90s, there were more and more homeless people who were not former day-laborers. They were accustomed to living in permanent dwellings and living on the street was a new and challenging experience. Moreover, these new homeless were having a hard time settling into the increasingly crowded public space. As Inaba, one of the members of the SRK, pointed out: 'More and more homeless would have a nomadic life, and street life was harder for them. Also, the question of trying to find a way out of the street was becoming more and more important' (Interview, March 2003)· Coming from a member of the Inoken, and thus a supporter of the community empowerment strategy, this comment is especially significant. It signals a change in their understanding of homelessness, a change which brought them back into an understanding with the Sogidan, whose members had reached the conclusion that they could not advance their agenda on employment policy and could no longer consider that living on the street was a viable solution (Interview, Honda san, May 2004). The final major obstacle to the inclusion policy, the TMG's non recognition of the SRK, would vanish in February 1998 when a fire destroyed the 'homeless village' in the Shinjuku underground. This was the community that had been constituted after the second eviction and was under the control of the SRK. The leaders not only felt a strong sense of responsibility for the death of four of their comrades and the destruction of the entire village, they also came to understand that living on the street was not safe. As Inaba explains: 'Until then, we were thinking that public space was not dangerous for homeless people. But after the fire, it was no longer possible to think in such a way' (Interview, March 2003).

The event also put pressure on the TMG, especially as the media and newspapers showed pictures and videos of the charred underground. TMG vowed to find a solution for those homeless people who had lost their cardboard houses. The solution they proposed took the shape of a shelter policy very similar to the one of 1996. A significant difference was that this time the SRK was included in the project and, by consequence, recognized as an official representative of homeless people's interests. The inclusion of the SRK members, who had the full confidence of the homeless, into the decision-making process brought success to the reinsertion policy. Eventually about 150 homeless people moved into a 200-bed shelter. This policy was supported entirely by the TMG during fiscal year 1999. Beginning in 2000, this local success was expanded via a full scale policy that included all 23 Tokyo wards. TMG, under the leadership of a new governor, coordinated its policies and actions with local homeless advocate organizations and implemented the first inclusive policy for homeless people called 'Centers for the support of the autonomy of homeless people' (See Figure 8.1). In subsequent years, the relation between the homeless support associations and local authorities would take an even more official turn as the 1998 NPO law was passed, providing NPOs with official recognition. Many of the organizations that had until then been struggling against the TMG would subsequently receive their NPO status from this very authority.

Conclusion

Though civil society is a broad term, I focused more specifically on the influence of two of its components: the local inhabitants' movement or what I referred to as the parochial mobilization and the radical left oriented homeless advocates' mobilization. Recent research has shown that both of these segments of civil society were less and less involved in the political process. Parochial mobilizations were concentrated on improving local community life, independently of the political field; the revolutionary agenda of radical left activists could not be integrated into the Japanese democratic system. However the case of Shinjuku demonstrates that homeless policy has been influenced by these actors of Japanese civil society. This politicization process goes against the mainstream idea of a non-political civil society dominated by volunteers. It shows that stronger attention should be given to traditional forces which have already influenced Japanese politics. They have adapted and they have their

Figure 8.1: Social inclusion policy—Support Center for Homeless Autonomy

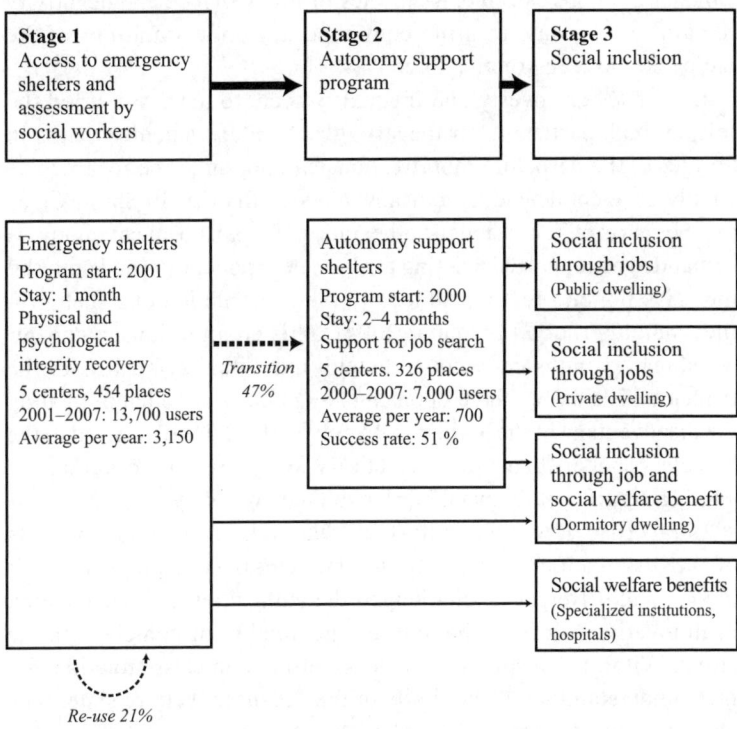

Source: Tokyo Metropolitan Government, 2008

own views and opinions about how to address the challenges that Japanese society will face in coming years.

The actions of both the parochial communities and the radical left activists have redefined these civil society actors in ways that challenge the mainstream views that developed from past actions. Since the 1970s parochial mobilizations mainly took the shape of amenity protest movements against environmental degradation and in defense of minorities. Challenging the Japanese model of growth, they were pointing out its sometimes tragic side effects, such as pollution and community destruction. With this history, parochial mobilizations have generally been understood as a positive force, warning about the limits of the system and its capacity to integrate citizens. In contrast, the massive mobilizations conducted by the radical left in the 1960s lost students and workers' support as they became increasingly more violent and more extreme. Memories of this violence and negativity remain vivid today, framing contemporary understandings of the radical left as a destructive force.

But issues of poverty and inequality seem to have reshuffled the roles of both parties. After the struggles to address homelessness in Shinjuku, the parochial mobilizations can no longer be regarded as simply an agent defending a disadvantaged minority. In Shinjuku, as in other parts of Tokyo and the other cities of Japan, local communities demanded or supported evicting the homeless population and opposed inclusive policies that would lead to the construction of a shelter in their neighborhood (Tsutsumi 2004). This communitarian egoism, which can paradoxically coincide with individual sympathy for the homeless, is a strong force opposing any policies aimed at mitigating the disadvantage of the homeless. In Tokyo, this NIMBYism led to the homeless shelters being displaced every five years, a process that has added a significant financial burden to the new policy.

In this case, it was the radical left that took action in the interests of the disadvantaged minority: the homeless. They put aside their ideological differences, challenged the authorities and participated in innovative solutions that curbed the number of homeless on the street. With their acquired knowledge of the homeless situation and their understanding of the limits of the Japanese welfare state, they have become partners of local authorities representing the civil society views on government committees focusing on the poverty issue. For instance, Yuasa Makoto and Inaba Tsuyoshi, both of whom have committed themselves to homeless advocacy since the 1990s, have been appointed to various government consultative committees. They support welfare, employment and housing policy reforms.

However, a new challenge is raising new concerns—not so much about the policies in place for assisting the poor, but about the definition of the poor in need of assistance. To date, homelessness in Japan has been narrowly defined by all actors to refer only to people who are on the street. However, since early 2000, NPOs have witnessed significant growth in the numbers of people living in new precarious conditions. They have been called 'internet café refugees' because they are not sleeping on the street but in 24-hour shops, the most common being 24-hour internet cafés which offer 'night packs' at much lower rates than the cheapest hotels. In contrast to the predominantly male and older homeless population, this new group is much younger and the gender distribution is more equal. Their problem is not that they have been excluded from the labor market but that they are only weakly integrated into it, moving from one non-regular job to another. From a sociological point of view, this can be understood as an extension of the growing problem of poverty in Japan. From a political point of view, it challenges the equilibrium between authorities and the various civil society actors regarding support for or opposition to the very poor. This might lead to a new mobilization process or alter the normative attributes of the existing ones.

9 Comparison of Poor People's Participation in Social Movements in France and Japan

Nanako Inaba

Introduction: A meeting of the Japanese and French social movements of the Have-nots (*les Mouvements des Sans*)

Synchronicity

It was shortly before Christmas in December 1994 when I discovered France's Right to Housing (*Droit au Logement*: DAL) movement as the homeless support groups DAL and CDSL (*Comité des Sans logis* [Homeless Committee]) and the jobless people's group AC! (*Agir Ensemble contre le Chômage!* [Action against Unemployment]) squatted in a vacant building at No. 7 *la rue du Dragon* in Paris. As 61 homeless families moved into the building occupied by the groups demanding the people's right to public housing with support from well-known intellectuals and artists and much media exposure, the incident raised awareness of the social exclusion problem in France. It ignited an active movement of the homeless, the jobless and undocumented foreigners who defined themselves as the Have-nots (*les Sans*).

At around the same time in 1994, a cardboard village of homeless people sprang up near the west entrance to Shinjuku train station in Tokyo. A majority of these men, who usually worked as day laborers on construction sites, had lost their jobs and housing in the midst of a recession and gathered at the semi-basement Shinjuku station square to take shelter from the weather. The number of cardboard box homes exceeded 300 at its peak. It has spawned many social movements.[1]

I was in France at the time to conduct research for my study on the DAL movement. My paper on DAL attracted much more interest from activists in the field than from academics, partly because of the absence of any concept of 'homeless movement' in Japan, and I was often invited to their seminars and workshops in the late 1990s. At the same time, I ended up taking on the role of a liaison between the French Right to Housing movement and the Japanese homeless movement and acting as an interpreter between them. The Japanese homeless movement at the time was comprised of groups supporting the homeless in traditional day laborers' areas such as Tokyo's Sanya district, Osaka's Kamagasaki district and Nagoya's Sasajima district based on construction day laborers' disputes as well as the groups in Tokyo's Shinjuku and Shibuya districts supporting the homeless who were working in new urban miscellaneous industries such as distribution.

To start with, Christophe Aguiton, an activist for the jobless movement, visited Japan in 1999. Japanese activists visited Paris in 2000 and galvanized exchanges with DAL, AC!, Droits devant!! and European March, which was organized against the Treaty of Amsterdam. When a group of the social movement organizations of the Have-nots led by DAL called for the establishment of the NoVox network (the network of the people who are deprived of a voice) at the European Social Forum in 2003, the Japanese movements in Sanya, Shibuya and Kamagasaki which had had contact with the French movements responded. Since then, the self-proclaimed Have-nots groups among Japanese homeless movement organizations have participated in the NoVox movement. Through these exchanges, Japanese and French Have-nots movements maintained frequent contact with one another.[2]

As I had conducted social surveys about the right to housing movement in Paris, I began to participate in comparative discussions as a mediator in both Japan and France from 2000. This chapter is based on the findings from these discussions as well as the results of the social surveys I conducted from 1994 by way of participant observation and interviews with activists participating in the right to housing and anti-unemployment movements and homeless and jobless individuals.

Composition of the chapter

The homeless movements in both Japan and France have a relatively short history as they became active from the 1990s. In Japan, homeless movements tend to head for involution and direct democracy by the homeless themselves, resulting in the formation of small homeless communities of their own. In France, however, the movements aim for integration into the general middle-class society rather than the formation of homeless communities. To explain this difference,

I will attempt to shed light on its cause by focusing on how activists have shaped these movements in relation to the homeless while taking into account some external conditions such as the social security situation and oppression of social movements. In particular, I will consider the process by which the homeless poor themselves become the actors of movements.

It is equally difficult in both Japan and France for the homeless to become the actors of movements. Both societies have been steeped in the meritocracy principle and accepted the myth of equality through school education.[3] In such societies, individuals are considered to be responsible for their own situations and they accept the responsibility. It is therefore difficult to articulate their circumstances in the form of a social movement. Nevertheless, social movements driven by the poor themselves have been formed in both Japan and France since the 1990s. How have the poor changed the interpretation of the poverty they have been experiencing and converted these interpretations into social movements? What were the social factors which prompted the poor in these similarly meritocratic societies to adopt different paths to express the poverty they were experiencing in the form of social movement?

First, we will consider the actors of movements. The main actors of France's right to housing movement are first-generation African migrants. Many of the actors of jobless movements are French people, including second and third-generation migrants with French nationality. By comparison, Japanese Have-nots movements were driven predominantly by single men until the mid-2000s. Second, we will look at the substance of their demands. While French Have-nots movements mainly demand the expansion of social security, including increased provision of public housing and unemployment benefits, Japanese movements concentrate on job creation. Third, we will compare alternative conceptions. Japanese movements reject capitalist society at the root of social exclusion and reject state intervention in everyday life in the community. Consequently, they tend to become critical of the middle-class life. By contrast, French movements seek integration into 'normal life' and do not necessarily develop into a criticism of the middle class. Is it the Japanese movements to which the word 'prophets' as used by Touraine (1991) applies? Finally, we will outline an impasse confronting Japanese movements and consider the future direction of the Have-nots movements.

The differences between Japanese and French movements presented in this chapter are findings from my empirical studies of a small number of organizations involved in the Have-nots movement and do not necessarily apply to all of the movements against social exclusion. Nevertheless, these organizations have played pioneering roles in the social movements against social exclusion in each country and I believe that a comparison between them will produce some arguments that may influence later movements against social exclusion. In Japan and France, there are many movements other than the social movement groups addressed in this chapter. However, those addressed in this chapter formed part of the 'anti-globalism' movement that became popular during the 2000s and, in addition to playing pioneering roles in the anti-social exclusion movement, have some of the characteristics of the anti-globalism movement, such as their emphasis on direct democracy and autonomy (Durand 2005). However, movements surrounding the same issue express themselves differently when the prevailing social conditions are different. This chapter attempts to compare them on the same platform in order to respond to the argument that French social movements have a large capacity to mobilize people while Japanese movements do not, which is raised every time French Have-nots movements by DAL and others are introduced in Japan. This is akin to arguing that direct action such as squatting is impossible in Japan due to 'cultural' differences between the Japanese and the French by looking at the outward expression of the movements. This type of reasoning fails to explain the fact that Japan had very active social movements during the 1960s and the 1970s. And assessing social movements on the basis of their mobilization capacity alone is a simplistic way of thinking. The actual meaning of the social movement is overlooked when it is judged superficially on the basis of the form of action or the number of participants.

Actors

Unstable employment

Anti-social exclusion movements in France increased from the 1990s, carried out by the homeless and the jobless themselves, demanding access to public housing by squatting in vacant buildings or the payment of minimum wages by voluntarily working at understaffed supermarket checkouts or post offices in the form of 'job squatting'. DAL is a movement run by families with children staying at hostels or otherwise having no fixed address almost consistently since its establishment in 1990, and AC! is a social movement by the jobless.

Japanese social movements in response to poverty began with movements to support the single male homeless during a slump in the construction sector. While the subsequent economic recession spawned young people's movements such as the Freeters' (casual workers) labor union, the movements against social exclusion have revolved around the sites of day laborers' movements such as Sanya and Kamagasaki. As the form of day labor changes, it has been observed that the movements need to demand livelihood protection and the right to a minimum standard of living rather than 'work'.

DAL is mainly driven by migrants. AC! is basically comprised of French people, including second and third-generation migrants. Day laborers in Japan are Japanese. However, such superficial differences are not very important. It is rather notable that this socially excluded class of people consists of workers in non-standard employment regardless of their nationality or race. The non-standard jobs are undertaken almost entirely by migrant workers in France and by Japanese workers in Japan. The class of people employed in the urban miscellaneous industries as construction workers, kitchen hands in restaurants, office cleaners, security guards, housekeepers in hotels, baby sitters and carers of the aged and sick are the actors of the Have-nots movements in France, and their jobs are 'migrants' jobs'. In Japan, the range of jobs for the Have-nots was not as broad at the beginning of the 1990s, but the addition of young casual workers called 'freeters' in recent years has broadened the base of this class of people. Still, those who are engaged in these jobs are 'Japanese' except in some manufacturing industries such as automobile, food and electrical.

So, what is the more important factor separating Japan and France? It is not their nationality or race. It is the degree to which 'society' is subsumed by the 'market'. With regard to housing, changes in labor conditions directly manifest as changes in the form of the movements surrounding social exclusion in the case of Japan. Many employers provide their employees with housing in Japan. Even temporary workers placed by agencies are provided with housing. And they lose access to housing unless they are employed continually. When they are in unstable employment moving from one urban sundry job to another, they cannot rent private rental accommodation.

In the pre-1995 period when temporary labor was strictly regulated in Japan, the homeless problem was limited to day-hire construction laborers. After temporary labor was deregulated in principle in all occupational categories in 1995, the population of young male temporary workers increased rapidly and the problem came to the surface as they had to vacate company dormitories immediately when their labor contracts were terminated. It is possible to say that these workers are forced to live on the street as soon as they lose their jobs because of the high degree to which 'society' is subsumed by the market in Japan.

In contrast, the right to a minimum standard of living is relatively independent of economic activity in France. Changes in the form of employment therefore do not change people's lives dramatically.[4] The 'homeless' are people with no fixed address but they are not necessarily living on the street. A majority of the actors of DAL have families and stay at hostels or friends' homes. Most of them are in unstable employment but they still earn the minimum wage. Some members of DAL are employed by the City of Paris as cleaners but are homeless because employment and housing are not connected. In other words, 'society' is not entirely subsumed by the 'market'.

Japan's Have-nots movements began with day laborers' movements but they gradually morphed into 'rough sleepers', or homeless, movements as hardly any jobs were available to men over the age of fifty by the mid-1990s. These men made a living by collecting aluminum cans and selling them to recycling companies.

The above descriptions may give rise to the suggestion that DAL cannot be compared with Japan's homeless. Perhaps the more literally defined French homeless, a majority of whom are single people, are more comparable to the Japanese homeless. However, many of the single homeless people living on the streets in France have mental problems or drug- or alcohol-induced illnesses and are in a different situation than Japan's single homeless people who demand to be integrated into society through 'work'.

The difference between Japan and France stems from the difference in the consequence of unstable employment. In France, temporary termination of unstable employment does not make the affected person homeless immediately. Daily-hire employment is prohibited by law. The situation of Japan's Have-nots is more similar to the situation of France's undocumented foreigners.

The internalization of self-responsibility and the difficulty of exercising one's right

The difference in the way the Have-nots are involved in their movements between France and Japan is attributable to the difference in their self-perception. A, an activist with the Sanya Day Laborers' Union, asks, 'Why can the Have-nots assert the Right to Housing and participate in direct action in France?' He wonders if it is because the French have the concept of demanding their rights, which is not the case for the Japanese. The actor who demands his 'right' comes into existence only when he perceives his existence positively and recognizes that it is worth exercising his right. In fact, DAL and AC! demand the security of housing and minimum income as legitimate basic rights (Mouchard 2002).

Japanese movements demand 'work' first. Housing comes with work. According to A, Japanese homeless movements have been fixated on the demand for 'work' instead of arguing that 'housing is a basic right' as the Right to Housing movement has been doing, because work alone forms the core of their identities. Many of the homeless in the Sanya Day Laborers' Union have repeatedly experienced failures in their lives. They have failed in interpersonal relationships, family relationships and marriages and cannot find any positive elements in their own lives. 'Work' is thus the only activity in which they can actually feel a sense of personal achievement.

As many of them work in the construction industry, the existence of buildings such as Tokyo Tower is the tangible result of their work and the only thing by which they perceive their own existence in a positive light. And society does not treat a jobless person with respect. Internally and externally, work forms part of the important foundation for one's identity as well as supporting oneself. That is why the demand for work takes the highest priority. Taking back work means taking back nothing less than their identity and dignity. Jobless people in Japan cannot even imagine that they could demand housing while being out of work.

The view that a jobless person is not a reputable adult has been internalized to this extent in Japan. Work is an important pillar of identity, especially for men. In fact, this line of thinking is common not only in Japan but also in the rest of the world. For this reason, women, young people or the unemployed who are placed outside of the working world have often been the actors of life-world-based movements. However, Japan's peculiarity lies in the fact that the life-world is dominated by corporations. Housing is often guaranteed by corporations, and work and housing are inseparable. People do not think that housing is part of social security, like medical care and education. Housing is something one gets as a result of work and one's housing reflects one's work. Owning a detached house is proof of one's success at work.

B talks about the homeless who live in shelters in parks and on river banks: 'They don't assert that it's a legitimate right as the French do. A majority of them are sorry for staying in a place where they are not supposed to stay'. C, another activist, says, 'They are not asserting the right to stay in the park; they ended up staying there after they were repeatedly treated with contempt when they applied for livelihood protection and thought, "I don't need this; I wouldn't take welfare payments even if they asked me to"'.

The homeless lose something that cannot be reduced to 'objects' such as a job or a house when they become jobless and homeless. They lose the foundation that supports their dignity. As I mentioned above, Japan's postwar history has been a process of corporations subsuming society. There is no place for those who are out of work. And those who are out of work not only have nowhere to live but also feel that they 'don't deserve to live'.

In contrast, 90 percent of those who are involved in the Right to Housing movement in and around Paris are migrant families, especially first-generation migrants, from former French colonies in West and North Africa who are engaged in urban bottom-rung labor. These migrant families feel less responsible for their poverty; they came to France to look for work because their native countries were poor in the first place. The migrants who came to France to escape poverty in their native countries are motivated to improve their living standards. Even among the urban bottom-rung workers, many working couples earn as much as 3,000 euro (420,000 yen) per month. There are sufficient conditions for them to feel that lack of access to private rental housing, not to mention public housing, is unjust.[5]

Jobless movements are driven by French people or second and third-generation migrants rather than first-generation migrants. Just like Japanese homeless movements, it has been more difficult for the Have-nots to become the actors of the movements than in the case of DAL. For example, APEIS[6] is a French movement for the jobless that made a grand appearance in the 1990s, but it had been active as a self-help organization to restore their dignity for almost ten years before that.

When actors feel that the validity of their existence is denied, it is difficult for them to actively participate in social movements. Jobless movements make a material demand for the higher guaranteed minimum wages and at the same time express their desire to be treated as individuals. For example, APEIS' slogans 'live', 'existence' and 'resistance' resonate with 'May day for Freedom and Existence' organized mainly by the Freeters' Union of Japanese youths in unstable employment or 'Let me be alive' asserted by the Collective House for Freedom and Existence.

Demands made by movements

Differences in marginalization

In the case of Japan, housing, which is directly linked to survival, is controlled by economic activity, especially corporations. The degree of exclusion is higher in Japan in that those who live in dormitories owned by employment agencies or companies in particular are forced to live literally on the street when they lose their jobs and homes. They become marginalized even after a short period of living on the street. The longer they live with no fixed address, the harder it gets for them to reintegrate into their previous lives (Snow 1993).

The biggest difference between the Japanese and French movements is the possibility of integration into the middle-class lifestyle. Since they are both Have-nots movements by nature, their goals are set proximate to something feasible and something they want. Most of the participants do not intend to make their social movements the main activity in their lives. They wish to lead a 'peaceful and normal' life.

If their realities are too far away to integrate into the middle-class lifestyle, they must find a new means of living outside of middle-class norms. The scope of movement also varies depending on whether the middle class considers it fair that the Have-nots attain the same standards of living as theirs.

It is extremely difficult to find a new means of living outside of the middle class. In the case of France, the Have-nots movements aim for integration into the middle-class lifestyle as symbolized by 'holding the key to one's own home' and their argument has the support of the general public. An alternative vision of a new society is pursued by young squatters who are not short of a place to sleep tonight, and they join forces with the Have-nots movements only when some important housing policy issues arise. In Japan, it is presumed that they cannot be accepted into the middle class due to a high degree of marginalization. For this reason, they inevitably look for an alternative somewhere outside of the middle-class lifestyle.

State intervention in the life world and social movements

The high degree of marginalization in Japan is not the only reason that Japanese movements give priority to an alternative goal. While the activists of Japanese homeless movements in the field were sympathetic toward the strategy of squatting in public spaces adopted by the French Have-nots movement, the most frequent question they asked was whether a strategy of demanding public housing or job creation is asking the state to intervene in civil society and whether this really constitutes a social movement.

'In the case of Southeast Asian movements, there is no concept of asking the state to do something for you, and people occupy a piece of land, build their own houses there and install electricity and water by themselves. Why do people ask the state to intervene in the case of France?'[7] D, who posed this question, was beginning to sell T-shirts at summer festivals or lunch boxes at academic seminars and symposiums on the newly spotlighted anti-poverty movement at the time in order to start up a business by the homeless instead of asking for welfare handouts. To him, 'social movement' means 'anti-authority' and 'anti-state'.

This is because the movements that have grown out of day laborers' movements have descended from the 1970s left-wing political movement which equates 'anti-authority' with 'anti-state' and has no notion of asking for state intervention. Even the later-formed movements, such as support organizations for tarpaulin shelter dwellers in parks, tend to operate based on the autonomy concept and tend to be repelled by any demands for a 'bigger state'.

The first project D undertook based on the autonomy concept was a 'food bank', which was to be operated independently, instead of asking the state for it. D then went on to set up a 'guarantor bank' as homeless people with no guarantors were unable to rent private accommodation. Now D is considering obtaining a qualification as a real estate agent so that they can start up their own real estate agency to find property owners willing to rent without guarantors, because it is extremely difficult to find such landlords.

E, who was involved in the founding of the food bank with D, began a recycling business in an attempt to break out of a situation in which he found it difficult to receive welfare benefits or get a new job. He sold recycled goods at first but he saw the limitations of their activity as a non-profit organization. He went on to set up a cooperative that operated house-moving, cleaning and recycling services.

This characteristic is not limited to the homeless movements formed during the 1990s. A group of young people in unstable employment led by the Freeters' Union founded the Collective House for Freedom and Existence in 2008 and renovated a dilapidated block of flats by themselves into a collective house.

This is where French and Japanese movements diverge. The French Have-nots movements have an orientation towards autonomy but they make the type of demand that requires the involvement of a bigger state. French activists unanimously affirm the movement's policy to appeal to the state by arguing as follows. Why is our demand for public housing regarded as state intervention? The state will not watch us inside our home. If the state will not give us housing, who else will? If the state will not do it, what is the use of the state? Our demand does not impose an excessive burden on the state; We ask the state to perform its redistribution function. It is a movement to seek justice by exposing whose money it is and who is making unfair profits.

An alternative: The creation of communality in the excluded space

Japanese 'society' is subsumed by corporations. A private space called housing is pervaded by corporations. One loses one's place to live in when one loses one's job. Without friends to rely on, one loses everything when one loses one's job. This situation was exposed by the increasing homelessness among young people in temporary employment during the financial crisis of 2008. In the present situation in Japan, one loses one's status as a 'person' as soon as one loses one's job. This problem cannot be solved by a return to the paternal and patriarchal 'Japanese management system' by which corporations try to protect workers and do not summarily dismiss them.

The more difficult it is to integrate into middle-class society the more inclined people become to find a new means to live. When the socially excluded are denied their 'personality' as well as experiencing material hardships, French movements pursue the possibility of having their identities recognized in mainstream society. As it is impossible in the case of Japan, Japanese movements pursue the possibility of having their identities recognized elsewhere. As they feel that their existence itself is being invalidated, they form a community of people in similar circumstances who recognize each other's existence. In Japan, tarpaulin tent villages in parks, for example, play the role of such a community.

F, an artist who voluntarily lives in a tent at a Tokyo park, talks about the 'joy' of his life. Of course, he does not deny the harshness of this life. However, he takes exception to the view that the homeless must continuously emphasize the misery and sufferings of their situation and that it is improper for them to find any joy in their lives. J talks about the joy of 'village' life, which is the joy of new communality.

H also lives in a park voluntarily after asking himself while he was involved in a homeless support movement as a student whether he wanted to follow the promised elite path after graduation from a university and end up on the side that kills the homeless. H also has a positive view of park dwelling and says that moving into a flat is not his goal because he regards the park dwellers' community as a place to nurture new communality.

We cannot conclude that F, J and H find the joy of communality only because they sleep rough in parks by choice. And we will overlook an important argument if we dismiss their talk of the joy of park dwelling as 'improper' in the light of their sufferings or as the switching of our focus away from the problem.

D points out that there were some homeless people who lived in a park during the 1990s and, after living in flats for a while, went back to living in the original tarpaulin village. As they worked from morning till night in order to pay the rent, then went home to eat alone, some of them began to ask if this lonely life was what they really wanted (even though living in a flat is definitely easier on the body). Getting a job and a flat does not make their life perfect. These observations suggest that the role of the tarpaulin tent village has changed from just a place to sleep in to a place where one has friends to affirm one's existence.

In France, this may happen as an action taken by individual activists but it is an improbable rationale for the Have-nots movement. Squatting in empty buildings is merely a means to an end, and not the place to experiment with new forms of communality. To DAL, squatting is not the solution. Their goal is to live in public housing and to literally hold the keys to their own homes. In this sense, the DAL activists do not deny that their pursuit is for integration into the mainstream society rather than a search for an alternative. According to L from DAL, 'Families come to DAL because they want to lead a normal life, not because they want to realize an alternative society'.

In other words, the participants' intention or desire to live within the bounds of 'normality' is respected. Since the degree of marginalization varies greatly depending on whether one has a home or not, the Right to Housing activists resist eviction and stress the importance of housing. They aim to avoid marginalization, striving instead to 'live like everyone else'.

Thus the alternative element of the early movement has been watered down in France because the demand for integration into mainstream society through public housing and higher minimum wages was more realistic.

However, the early concept of 'society without unemployment' had an alternative element according to M, who was involved in the founding of AC! This 'alternative' was regarded as 'dangerous' by the authorities. AC! subsequently became a Have-nots movement and its 'action is radical but argument is fair' just like many of the other Have-nots movements according to M's assessment. They demand to 'live like a normal person'. L from DAL makes a similar point. 'The DAL movement is acknowledged by the government, which is prepared to negotiate with us. It is because everyone understands our argument that it is unjust for families working diligently not to be able to get public housing. Even though our direct action is radical, we can still attract sympathy from the general public because we are not planting a bomb on a bus.'

The future of the alternative: Involution

In that case, does the Japanese Have-nots movement have a viable idea for the future? The matter is not that simple. Not being accepted by the mainstream society may make the newly created space of communality an inwardly closed community. In particular, a lifestyle that rejects capitalism or the oppression of others may not be feasible unless the community breaks away from mainstream society in some cases. If people can form a community by connecting with fellow members who recognize one another's existence, respect one another as equals and share the same values, the socially excluded may end up forming a closed space that excludes the people who exclude them.

Moreover, the building of a new community means that individuals belong to some type of order (an affinity group in this case) by their own efforts, and this integration from below by self-supporting efforts is convenient for the system. As Dubet points out, a social movement is also reclaimed by the question of how to mobilize various resources, communities, public opinion and networks and is not merely an expression of conflicts with the establishment. In fact, it is recognized as compatible with the establishment in some cases (Dubet 2009: 161).

Not only the discourses but also the actions of the DIY (Do It Yourself) Movement spreading among young people and the cooperatives formed by the Have-nots appear to mark the realization of an alternative, but they may become closed and self-contained spaces founded on the principle of autonomy. They frequently choose a lifestyle which avoids the traps of consumerism in order to avoid taking part in capitalism, be it collecting dumped items, not throwing things away, DIY repair, recycling or 'free price'. Even so, it is undeniable that simply 'breaking away' from the capitalist system is no more than living quietly in a community of social dropouts who understand each other and this situation is rather convenient for the system. This is the impasse facing the Have-nots movements.

10 Employment at All Costs? Limits and Shortfalls of French Employment Policies

Pierre Concialdi

In France, as in many other countries, unemployment has been a massive and persistent feature of the labor market for more than three decades. However, employment remains a key issue for the social integration of people. In order to slow the rise of unemployment or even reduce it, public authorities started to implement employment policies in the 1970s. In this area, France was probably one of the first countries to begin the development of these policies. It is also a country which has implemented a very large range of employment policies.

The objectives of these policies, their rationale and the measures used to implement them greatly changed in the 1990s. Previous policies targeting specific categories of the population and aiming either at facilitating their insertion in the labor market, or at making unemployment socially more sustainable gradually gave way to more general policies. These general policies were centered essentially on reducing labor costs and sharing the hours worked, especially through an increase in part time work. This trend towards more general employment policies came along with a degradation of employment standards. As a consequence, precarious employment and contingent jobs increased, leading to greater vulnerability of working people. The latest development of these general policies is the creation in June 2009 of the RSA (*Revenu de solidarité active)*, which is likely to reinforce these trends.

The aim of this paper is to analyze the main characteristics of these changes (section 1) and to try to assess their consequences on the functioning of the labor market and the related consequences on the living conditions of employees (section 2). In the final section, we discuss the relevance of these policies in combating the social exclusion that originates from unemployment.

Employment policies: A brief outline

Specific employment policies began to be developed in the 1970s, with the implementation of three categories of measures targeting three specific populations:

Measures concerning older workers were implemented very early to facilitate and encourage the withdrawal from the labor market of the oldest employees threatened with redundancy. In the 1980s, the number of people affected by these measures increased very rapidly with the development of pre-retirement schemes. In the mid-1980s, new measures were introduced to allow older age job-seekers to continue to receive their unemployment allowances without any conditions for actively seeking a job. Measures concerning young job-seekers were implemented in the 1970s and targeted the least qualified of them (training courses, exemptions from employers' social contributions for those hiring them, vocational training, etc). Since the mid-1980s, other measures were introduced for long-term unemployed.

For young people and the long-term unemployed, these specific employment policies were mainly aimed at boosting their employment opportunities to compensate for their disadvantages in the labor market. For older workers, the main objective of the measures was to provide some form of income support to people who were considered to have few chances of finding employment before reaching retirement age. Pre-retirement schemes were an efficient tool to achieve this goal. The assessment might be more mitigated for older unemployed people exempted from any active job search. Overall, these employment policies tried to organize transitional statutes, either towards stable jobs (young people, long term unemployed), or towards retirement (older workers).

In the late 1980s and early 1990s, several measures were taken that initiated a change of orientation of employment policies. The objective of these new measures was no longer to compensate for the disadvantages of certain categories of the population in the labor market nor to support these populations, but to encourage certain types of employment. This was done through exemptions from employers' social contributions or various forms of fiscal subsidies.

Exemptions from employers' social contributions for part-time jobs were implemented in 1992.[1] This is the most significant measure of this new period. The idea that came in the front of the political agenda was no longer to fight unemployment, but to organize some form of job-sharing. In the following year, 1993, the first exemptions from employers' social contributions for so called "low wage jobs" were introduced. Since then, this measure has widened. Today, it concerns more than 60 percent of employees.[2]

There are three main differences between these new general measures implemented in the early 1990s and previous employment policies:

- These measures do not target specific categories of employees (labor supply); they are aimed at encouraging specific types of jobs (labor demand);
- Measures are permanent and not limited in time;
- They do not concern unemployed people, but employees who already have a job.

With the election in 1997 of a new socio-democratic government, two measures modify these priorities: the "Youth Employment Plan" and the reduction of the legal working time to 35 hours per week. The "Youth Employment Plan" can partially be analyzed as a specific measure insofar as it concerns young people under the age of 25. However, two distinctive features of this plan are very different from previous measures targeting young people. First, the plan is intended to create new jobs in order to satisfy social needs. Second, the plan does not target less qualified young workers as was mainly the case previously. The aim of the "35 hour" week is clearly to increase the number of jobs available on the labor market through a collective measure.[3] In sum, both measures are intended to create new jobs rather than to organize some form of redistribution of jobs already available.

A radical shift in employment policies was taken in January 2001 with the implementation of the PPE (*Prime pour l'emploi*). The PPE is a means tested tax credit that supplements the incomes of low wage earners. The means test is based on household incomes whereas the "wage test" is individual. It is calculated as a percentage of earned income and either deducted from the income tax to be paid or paid directly to the beneficiary if s/he is not taxable. This measure is coherent with the exemption from employers' social contributions on low wage jobs. With these exemptions, employers are encouraged to develop these "poor jobs" and, with the PPE, employees are granted direct incentives to accept these jobs. In other words, the aim of this policy is no longer to make unemployment socially acceptable with the creation of transitional statutes to regular jobs with the prospect of full employment. The implicit assumption of this policy is that one

Table 10.1: Main characteristics of employment policies

	Targeted policies	**General policies**
Objectives	To compensate for some specific disadvantages on the labor market To make unemployment socially sustainable	To share employment Action on labor costs to stimulate employment
Main characteristics of measures	Transitory measures towards: regular employment retirement	Permanent measures
Targeted population	Unemployed and people facing specific difficulties in the labor market (older people, young people with poor qualifications, etc)	Employed people
Measures	Specific contracts Exemptions of employers' social contributions in specific cases Traineeship, education Preretirement schemes and other special schemes for old age unemployed	Exemptions of employers' social contributions Part time work Low wage employment Reduction of working time Fiscal subsidies to low wage workers and working poor

must be resigned to the fact of mass unemployment and to deal with its related consequences (low salaries, precarious jobs), which are supposedly now a permanent feature of the labor market.

The RSA, created in December 2008 and effective from June 2009, goes a step further in the same direction. The RSA substitutes for previous minimum income guarantees.[4] However, its main characteristic is that it is also a means tested tax credit that supplements the incomes of the beneficiaries when they hold (or find) very low wage jobs. The upper limit for the means test (based on household incomes) is far above the level of the minimum guaranteed income. So it is expected that a large number of the so called "working poor" (approximately 2 million people), whose household incomes are higher than the minimum income, will still get this tax credit. Today, only 400,000 "working poor" receive this benefit.

In this respect, the PPE and the RSA have very similar features and the RSA can be considered as an extension of the PPE to very low wage earners. These two devices share two common points:

- The PPE and the RSA confirm the idea that it is possible, not to say desirable, that employees may have a job which does not allow them a decent standard of living.
- Both measures identify a public characterized mainly by individuals who are capable of taking advantage of market resources, in this particular case of the labor market.

The following figure summarizes the main characteristics of the employment policies, both targeted and general ones.

Issues and debates

One can identify several factors that have led to this fundamental reorientation of employment policies.

Targeted measures have been criticized for a long time because of some well-known effects (windfall effects, substitution effects) (Daniel 1998). However, it is also necessary to underline the fact that the logic of these measures is cumulative: identifying new populations with employment problems does not mean that the other forms of disadvantage have disappeared. Therefore there has been an accumulation over the years of a variety of measures. With the persistence of mass unemployment, the idea progressively emerged that everything, or almost everything, had been tried to fight unemployment and that these targeted measures could no longer be the only answer.

In this context, a compromise was formed between, on one hand, the neo-Keynesian economists worried about protection tools such as the SMIC (guaranteed minimum wage) in order to preserve social cohesion and, on the other hand, the neo-liberal economists for whom the main worry was to reduce labor costs and to increase profits. This compromise led to the implementation of exemptions from employers' social contributions on "low wage jobs", thus allowing lower labor costs (the neo-liberals' objective) without decreasing the gross salaries earned by employees (the neo-Keynesian objective).[5]

Various forms of subsidies to employers (i.e. exemptions of employers' social contributions) were introduced in the latter half of the 1990s. During the same period, the second part of the neo-liberal thesis became increasingly prominent in the public debate, namely the idea that unemployment is voluntary and results from the individual making a rational choice between the proposed salary and the social-security benefits received. This is part of the long running debate over the question of the disincentive effects of social transfers. Within the three years (1998–2000) that preceded the implementation of the PPE, this debate was fuelled by no less than a dozen reports or studies, released mainly by government bodies. It might be stretching it to draw a direct link between this heated debate on the disincentive effects of social transfers and the changes that have been observed in public opinion. Nevertheless, it is clear that public opinion towards the poor changed during the same period. Following the creation of the general minimum guaranteed income (RMI) in 1988, a large majority of people (approximately two out of three) agreed with the statement that the RMI "provides necessary support to help poor people." Support for this view slowly dissipated over time. Since 2000, public opinion towards people on welfare has changed dramatically. A majority of persons now consider that the minimum guaranteed income "risks inciting people to settle with it and might be a disincentive to look for a job".

These reports on the alleged disincentive effects of social transfers were not based on specific studies looking at the actual behavior of people living on the RMI. They were only based on the comparison of the disposable income for people living on the RMI, on one hand, and the disposable income of people living on a low wage job, on the other hand. It is worth noting that these reports were systematically biased insofar as they always ignored the fact that, when a beneficiary of the RMI found a job, s/he could always still get part of his/her previous benefit for up to one year. In other words, there was always a financial interest for unemployed living on the RMI to take a job, at least for one year.

However, since the minimum wage is an hourly wage rate, the minimum income always equals a given number of hours paid at this minimum wage, which today roughly equals a half-time job. Therefore, it is not surprising that so many reports have concluded that people living on the RMI had no financial incentive to work on such jobs. These reports have helped to promote a new employment standard: the half-time SMIC.

The implementation of the RSA confirms this representation and this new standard. The RSA indeed distinguishes two categories of beneficiaries. Those whose earned income is lower than 500 Euros per month (the equivalent of a half-time SMIC) have to sign a "contract of mutual commitment" which automatically pushes them, in most cases, towards public employment agencies (*Pôle Emploi* today). The law on the "rights and duties of the job-seekers" enacted in 2008 is very likely to force these beneficiaries to lower their wage claims at the risk of being disqualified.[6] A kind of French-style workfare is being set up with this mechanism. At the same time, the beneficiaries whose earned income is above 500 Euros a month are not bound to the same obligation. The half-time SMIC has thus become the new administrative standard for classifying and sorting unemployed people.

The representations and theoretical foundations associated with employment policies have changed profoundly over the past thirty years. Until the 1990s, the main idea was that unemployed people were above all victims of the economic crisis that followed the oil crises of the 1970s. With the reduction of the unemployment benefits and the tightening of the entitlement conditions at the beginning of the 1980s, more and more unemployed people were left without any kind of income support. This led, in 1988, to the creation of the RMI in order to mitigate the shortcomings of the unemployment insurance scheme. Year after year, mainstream representations switched towards the idea that unemployed people are "responsible" for their unemployment, in the sense that it is rational for them to refuse any employment paying less than the guaranteed minimum income or, more generally, than the transfers which they receive.

The theoretical framework associated with this representation of unemployment problems is a very simplified one. On one hand, unemployment is supposed to be the consequence of an "excessive" labor cost. It is therefore necessary to lower labor costs to boost employment with employment subsidies (such as exemptions from employers' social contributions) in order to provide companies with greater incentives to create jobs. On the other, the existence of a minimal safety net is supposed to be a disincentive for unemployed people to take a job, and it is therefore necessary to provide unemployed people with financial incentives (subsidies), which encourage them to "get back" to employment. In this logic, market prices are the key factor of the regulation of the labor market, with almost no limits on the decline of wages. If lowering labor costs does not result in a significant rise in employment (or decline in unemployment), one can always conclude that it is necessary to further reduce labor costs and, as a consequence, wages. This is now made possible with measures such as the RSA and there is thus no limit on the continuous and general reduction in wages as long as the labor market is characterized by massive unemployment. In the context of the current global financial crisis, one can logically expect that this process will gain in importance and that employers will take advantage of these measures to put more and more pressure on wages.

We shall not discuss here the soundness of these theoretical foundations. However, as for any public policy, the main question is an empirical one concerning their efficacy. There were no great difficulties in answering this question in the case of targeted employment policies. Considering the number of beneficiaries, the cost of the measures or both indicators, analysts could assess their results. To assess the efficacy of the "new" employment policies based on general incentives is, on the contrary, much more difficult. Theoretically, one could consider that someone who found a job thanks to this policy would be a "beneficiary" of a general employment policy (such as the exemptions from employers' social contributions on "low wage jobs"). But it is clearly very difficult to identify these beneficiaries. Because of the lack of easily measurable physical indicators, evaluation studies are at the core of the debate on the efficacy of general employment policies. The controversies that surrounded the publication of the first evaluations of the experiments of the RSA are a clear illustration of this situation.

Assessment of employment policies

What can we say about the efficacy and the relevance of the general employment policies that have been implemented since the early 1990s? Depending on the level of analysis, several answers can be offered.

The assessment of the general employment policies carried out since the early 1990s (whether with regard to the exemptions from employers' social contributions or the reduction of working hours) has been very controversial for many years. In the past few years, however, two statements seem to have become rather consensual. First, the "35 hour week" would have created between 300,000 and 500,000 jobs (Husson 2002; IRES 2009: ch.1). Second, subsidies to "low wage jobs" would have created or protected approximately 100,000 jobs (Rémy 2005). There is no doubt that the reduction of working hours has had a stronger impact on employment than the reduction in labor costs. The action on the duration of work (and consequently on the number of jobs) is more decisive than the action on the price of labor. This is clearly illustrated by the attitude of employers' organizations that strongly support subsidies for low wage jobs whereas they are strongly opposed to any change in the legal norms concerning the hours of work, even though the "35 hour week" did not hamper the competitiveness of French companies.

Globally, however, these employment policies did not succeed in reducing unemployment. Since the mid-1980s, mass unemployment has become a structural feature of the French labor market. Unemployment ranges from eight to ten percent depending on specific economic circumstances. Moreover, the number of underemployed people has increased significantly. Underemployment figures since the early 1990s are available through the Labor Force Surveys. Despite some methodological and conceptual changes,[7] one can estimate that the number of underemployed people has more than doubled since the early 1990s, increasing by one million. In other words, not only did unemployment not decline but underemployment increased considerably.

In this context of persistent unemployment, the number of precarious or part-time jobs has increased dramatically since the early 1980s: temporary work increased five times, fixed term contracts four times, subsidized part time jobs three times and the underemployed population doubled. All in all, the number of precarious jobs increased by 2.5 million between 1983 and 2005. This increase represents more than 60 percent of the total growth of employment (four million) during the same period.

This trend came along with increasingly precarious earned incomes. The most visible sign of this phenomenon is the sharp increase in the proportion of low wage jobs (below two-thirds of the median wage; i.e., approximately 90 percent of the full-time monthly minimum wage). This proportion increased from 11.4 percent in 1983 to 17.7 percent in 1998. During the period 1998–2002, France experienced the sharpest increase in employment over the past 60 years and the percentage of low wage jobs fell slightly to 16.2 percent in 2002. Since then, the proportion of low-wage jobs is likely to have increased again. At the same time, the number of "working poor" has also increased.

The alleged political aim of subsidies for low wage jobs (for employers as well as employees) is to facilitate access to regular full time jobs. However, the various studies carried out on this issue can hardly identify any significant effect that these measures have had on access to regular jobs. One recent econometric study (Givord and Wilner 2009) concludes that there is a "light springboard" short-term effect for a minority of temporary jobs. On the contrary, various

Table 10.2: Percentage of the labor force that is either on a low wage job or unemployed during three years

	1983–85	1990–92	1998–00
At least one year on a low wage job or unemployed [1]	19.6	22.6	30.1
Always on a low wage job or unemployed [2]	7.3	9.3	16.7
Of which :			
Always on a low wage job	3.5	4.8	7.8
Either on a low wage job or unemployed	1.3	2.3	3.5
Always unemployed	2.5	2.2	5.4
Indicator of persistence [2]/[1]	37.2	41.1	55.5

Source: INSEE, Labor Force Surveys

studies document the low wage trap phenomenon (Guillemot et al. 2002). Since the early 1980s, more and more employees are trapped in situations combining periods of unemployment and periods of short term employment.

Indeed, along with the growth in low wage jobs one can also observe an increase in the risk of being—at least in the short term (3 years)—stuck in low wage jobs. At the same time, shifts between unemployment and low wage jobs have become more frequent. All in all, among all those who participated in the labor market in three successive years, the proportion who were always either on low wage jobs or unemployed more than doubled over fifteen years. It was 7.3 percent in the period 1983–1985 and 16.7 percent in 1998–2000 (Table 10.2). The increase was particularly strong in the 1990s when new employment policies were implemented.

Despite the fact that, as Atkinson and Mogensen (1993: 296) put it, "Disincentives associated with welfare benefits may be irrelevant at times of high unemployment," there has been a heated debate on this issue since the late 1990s. There is a large economic literature on the issue of poverty traps and/or unemployment traps. The disincentive effect of social transfers is often taken for granted in this literature. However, as Atkinson (1983: 422) notes: "There is no theoretical necessity that there must be a disincentive effect ... The *existence* of a disincentive effect, and not merely its magnitude, is a matter for empirical demonstration." The numerous reports and studies in France that focused on this issue in the late 1990s were not empirical studies (see above). Furthermore, they only valued employment by the wages associated with it. This simplistic way of reasoning is far from being established by studies based on surveys conducted with the beneficiaries of minimum incomes.

According to a survey with the beneficiaries of basic welfare benefits, 72 percent of them actively seek a job (Belleville-Pla 2004). Among the 28 percent that do not look for employment, 40 percent mention problems of health and only five percent declare that "to work would not be of financial interest." These results are in line with those of a previous survey with the beneficiaries of the RMI, which studied the trajectory of these beneficiaries over 18 months (Guillemot *et al.* 2002). The authors summarize the main results of the study as follows:

> First, recipients who are unemployed are very active in job searching and rarely refuse a job and even more rarely for financial reasons. They are more likely to face a shortage of labor demand. Secondly, about one out of three recipients who have accepted a job, do so with no financial advantage. For most of them, however, employment provides enhanced well-being. The risk for RMI recipients is more that of falling into a poverty trap than into an unemployment trap. Indeed, they most often have "poor quality jobs" and remain confined to a secondary sector, with a very low probability of migration towards a primary sector composed of "high quality jobs". (Guillemot *et al.* 2002: 1235)[8]

In other words, there is no unemployment trap but, as previously discussed, there is a low wage trap.

More generally, it is necessary to emphasize that there is no miracle solution to the issue of disincentive effects. With a system of tax credits, it is always possible to increase incentives to "work more" for people at the lowest end of the wage distribution. However, there is always a limit above which the incentives must decrease so that there is no tax credit above a given threshold. The consequence is that there are always positive as well as negative effects on the labor supply. Studies carried out in the US concerning the EITC (Earned Income Tax Credit) show that the net effect on employment is marginal. In other words, the main effect of tax credits is to operate a kind of "redistribution" of employment among people who are eligible for the tax credit. The problem is that this redistribution is confined to the most vulnerable part of the population.

In France, such tax credits would not be the right answer to employment problems faced by workers. A comparison of poor workers in France and the United States has clearly underlined this fact (Concialdi and Ponthieux 2000). In France, poor earned income is essentially the result of both short weekly hours being offered and spells of unemployment during the year. By contrast, in the United States, poor earned income is related more to low hourly rates of pay.[9] Therefore, if the aim is to improve workers' living conditions, it seems more sensible, and indeed more appropriate in France to promote new safeguards enabling part-time workers to pursue their employment activities full-time if they so wish. Naturally, such an approach would not dispel the need to pursue an active policy on minimum earnings, as these two levers are complementary. Otherwise, policies pursued since the 1990s in France that aim to encourage employment run serious risks, not only of having a limited effect in terms of creating jobs, but also of causing further erosion of workers' living standards. In other words, we would end up with all the disadvantages of both the European and American "models" and none of the advantages.

The conclusion of this study clearly underlined that risk:

> Such provisions hardly seem appropriate in the case of France... Paradoxically, therefore, the introduction of similar provisions to support the low-paid in France could lead, in the medium and long term, to erosion in the relative level of the guaranteed minimum wage, or indeed to its abolition, as some employers are demanding. In the long term, such a measure could undermine the entire edifice of social protection measures painstakingly built up over the last two centuries. (Concialdi and Ponthieux 2000: 670)

Some concluding remarks

While the global financial crisis that erupted in 2008 clearly underlined the limits of market mechanisms, these mechanisms are still at the heart of French employment policies. These policies have not succeeded in fighting unemployment. However, they might well increase poverty and lead more and more workers into dead-end jobs, a trend that will exacerbate social antagonisms. Indeed, public employment policies that were implemented over the past twenty years not only weakened the situation of a growing proportion of employees, but also increased the competition between employees.

These changes reflect fundamental changes in the rationale for social protection. While the initial intention of social protection systems was to create protections that supplemented the salary and contributed to build an employee's status, it tends to become more and more a substitute for the salary. At the same time, workers tend to be exclusively defined by their capacity to take advantage of labor market resources. Fiscal subsidies to poor employees are the most visible example of this radical change. However, the increasing number of possibilities for supplementing social-security benefits with wages (for unemployed people and retired people) goes in the same direction. This is especially the case in a period when decreasing benefits might well force an increasing proportion of beneficiaries (particularly among retired people) to supplement low pensions by supplementary earned income.

The Fordist period was characterized by macroeconomic policies aimed at full employment, which is one of the key issues for Social Security as emphasized by Beveridge (1944).[10] The crisis which started in the 1970s led to a situation where one can say that social protection tends today to have become an instrument of a "discounted" full employment, where most vulnerable people have to, or even might be obliged to share employment crumbs.

11 When Law is Facing Poverty: Looking for a New "Adjudicative Space" for Social Rights

Isabelle Giraudou

Introductory remarks: Law *in the Face of* Poverty

Law has been slow to take poverty into account. So far the legal world has only produced a small number of scholars specializing in this issue, and for a long time law envisaged poverty either under assistance or repression oriented mechanisms—to protect social order against the perceived menace associated with the presence of poor populations. Above all, if poverty has been the object of special and various interventions, it never formed a legal category in the real meaning of the term. Considering only some aspects of poverty, law has never really conceived of poverty as such. It is paradoxical that despite recurrent debates in various political forums, no legal definition of poverty has ever been elaborated. The progressive 'juridification' of all these discussions means that positive law does not fully acknowledge the phenomenon. In law, poverty appears only indirectly (through, for example, the notion of needs). So that, rather than any notion of "poverty *in* French law", it would be more relevant to speak about "French law *in the face of* poverty". The question is therefore to know how, how far and on which basis law addresses poverty related problems.

More precisely, in recent years several legal initiatives have been taken which contribute to renewing the legal answers to such problems. Legal measures adopted to fight against poverty do not aim exclusively at preserving social cohesion, as in the past, but are also and above all focused on the necessity to protect the fundamental rights of those who are vulnerable because of poverty. In other words, poverty is apprehended negatively as a situation in which a citizen with rights is deprived of the enjoyment of his or her fundamental rights. But a paradox remains: if the necessity to guarantee social rights is acknowledged, legal discourse continues to make a distinction between economic, social and cultural rights on the one hand, and civil and political rights on the other.

The following essay, which consists of a slightly augmented version of the presentation given in October 2010, describes the successive steps by which French law in particular has progressively reinforced the protection of fundamental social rights. However, acknowledging the legally binding character of these rights (or to say it in French, their *juridicité*) is one thing; fully consecrating the possibility for rights holders to claim effective protection and remedy before the court (or "justiciability") is another. In France too, if the former has become indisputable, the latter is still debated.

Recognition of the legally binding character of socio-economic rights

The idea that individuals possess a (constitutional) right to claim minimal assistance as well as education from the State was first conceptualized by the revolutionaries who ruled in 1793. But it was under the influence of socialist criticism and the willingness of the major political forces after World War II to define a new social contract that the political imperative to give constitutional recognition to a new generation of human rights, the so-called social rights, emerged. The Preamble of the Constitution of 1946 emphasizes the collectivity as the new "debtor" of the rights guaranteed in various paragraphs,[1] all of which were conceived as embodying social rights belonging to the *"droits-créances"* category and, as such, implying as a matter of principle positive action from public authorities. Such a view is still the dominant one today (even if the definition of *"droit-créance"* lacks precision and is likely to differ from scholar to scholar).

However, by labeling social rights as *"droits à..."* (or rights to) as opposed to *"droits de..."* (or rights of),[2] a number of French scholars have tended to systematically associate *"droits-créances"* with constitutional objectives or principles, and for this reason deny their justiciable character—as if a *"droit-créance"* should *per se* exclude the quality of subjective rights. These authors have deplored the fact that the programmatic nature of such rights undermines the concept of subjective rights.[3] Some, in their attempt to deny the legal nature of the principles enunciated by the 1789 Declaration and the 1946 Preamble (which both are embodied in the Constitution of the Fifth Republic) even suspected these rights of weakening the overall concept of human rights itself.[4]

The 1971 landmark ruling by the Constitutional Council dramatically altered such attempts. Both the 1789 Declaration and the 1946 Preamble have been recognized as statements of constitutional value—so that any violation of their provisions would cause a statute to be invalidated. Since the so-called *Liberté d'association*[5] ruling, it is well established that all constitutional norms, including the fundamental rights recognized by the Constitution and protected by the constitutional judges, are at the same normative hierarchical level. There is no longer any doubt that the positive socio-economic rights guaranteed by the 1946 Preamble is legally binding on all public authorities. However, "constitutionalization" appears somewhat limited. In fact, "juridicity" (or the legally binding character of such rights) is one thing, "justiciability" another. If the former became indisputable, the latter is still debated. And the Constitutional Council appears quite reluctant to strictly scrutinize any law involving "*droits-créances*". Considering the question of the justiciability of social rights from both a theoretical and a pragmatic perspective, we first review some of the major general concerns raised in relation to whether such rights can, or should be, adjudicated by courts, before concentrating on the situation in French law.

Rights without claimants? The general problem of justiciability

International human rights law as well as a number of domestic legal systems provide for the protection of fundamental social and economic rights (such as the right to health, housing, food and labor-related rights). However, and since the separation of the integrated rights in the *Universal Declaration of Human Rights* into two Covenants, questions about the justiciability of economic, social and cultural rights have dogged the international human rights movement. Compared to civil and political rights, the inferior status of economic and social rights has for many years had a negative impact on the possibility of claiming effective protection of these rights at both the international and domestic levels. In practice, it remains difficult to denounce a violation of an economic or social right before a court of law, and their justiciability is still being debated.

"Justiciability"—or the right to a remedy for a violation—means that people who claim to be victims of violations of these rights are able to file a complaint before an independent and impartial body to ask for adequate remedies if a violation has been found to have occurred or to be likely to occur, and to have any remedy enforced. Justiciable rights grant right-holders a legal course of action to enforce them each time the duty-bearer does not comply with his or her duties. Legal remedy is understood both in the sense of providing a procedural remedy (effective access to an appropriate court or tribunal) when a violation has already occurred or is imminent, as well as the process of awarding adequate reparation to the victim. As such, the right to a remedy (either under the form of preventive measures, injunctions, monetary compensation, or administrative penalties or criminal punishment, etc) has often been considered one of the most fundamental rights for the effective protection of all other human rights.

Ongoing debate

The discussion about whether social rights can or should be adjudicated and enforced by courts or other bodies is not new. In fact, such a debate has been going on since the 1960's, when the rights in the *Universal Declaration of Human Rights* were divided into two separate covenants—one containing economic, social and cultural rights (which commits the 155 state parties to work *towards* granting of ESCR to individuals), while the other set out civil and political rights.[6] Although both sets of rights were affirmed to be indivisible and interdependent, commentators have often distinguished between the two categories of rights—the justiciability of the second category of rights still being a matter of dispute.

Doctrinal works that deny the justiciability of social rights tend to rely more specifically on three primary arguments. According to these commentators, social as well as economic and cultural rights—which include an adequate standard of living, freedom from hunger, education, and the highest attainable standard of health—are different in nature from civil and political rights. For this very reason, these rights are non justiciable. Unlike civil and political rights, social rights are said to give rise to positive duties (to respect, protect and fulfill) rather than imposing negative ones. In other words, if States are required to refrain from interfering with the enjoyment of social and economic rights, they have to take measures that prevent third parties from interfering with the enjoyment of such rights and to take steps to facilitate individuals and communities enjoying these rights (or to provide what is necessary for this enjoyment). As such, social rights require government action rather than government restraint, allocation of resources and progressive realization rather than immediate compliance, and are characterized by vagueness, openness and indetermination (e.g. right to adequate standard of living) rather than by precision and legal definitions.

Another claim expressed by the same commentators is that it remains undemocratic, if not anti-democratic or "counter-majoritarian" for unelected courts to interfere with administration of the public purse and social and economic policy adopted by elected branches of government (the "legitimacy" concern); it is also feared that the possibility of courts dealing with social and economic rights will result in a violation or a distortion of the traditional balance associated with the separation of powers among the three branches or organs of government (the legislature, the executive and the judiciary).

Finally, they pretend that social and economic rights involve complex issues (such as the difficulty of achieving consensus regarding applicable or minimum standards) and competing claims on resources which courts have no capacity to properly adjudicate (the "competency" concern).

Even if an increasing number of countries include social and economic rights in their constitutions, and domestic courts[7] as well as regional bodies[8] routinely adjudicate and rule upon social and economic rights claims, the debate about the trends and challenges of demanding social and economic rights through judicial means is not over; it is indeed reviving since the 1990s in different countries and regions, as well as at an international level.

In particular, the recent discussions at the United Nations about an optional protocol to establish a complaints mechanism for the International Covenant on Economic, Social and Cultural Rights (ICESCR) has shown that there remains resistance to recognizing the full justiciability of social and economic rights on the part of some states. Since it has become much more difficult over time to persist with serious arguments that these rights are not justiciable, states less in favor of an optional protocol (such as Australia, the USA and the UK) have tried to avoid any simple opposition; after having replaced the debate about *whether* economic and social rights are justiciable with discussions on *how* these rights ought to be adjudicated, a significant number of state delegations continued to argue that, in order to limit the "scope and application" of any complaints procedure, they strongly favored a provision which would allow states to pick and choose "*à la carte*" which rights or aspects of rights should be subject to adjudication.[9] Arguing this way, the reluctant states raised a set of questions: how far to go in creating institutional mechanisms for the adjudication and enforcement of social and economic rights; how to delimit the role of courts or other bodies in adjudicating those rights; and how to determine the relationship of such institutional mechanisms with the elected branches of government?

But fundamentally, and from the perspective of those whose rights are at stake, the critical question is how to ensure governments' accountability to human rights norms: in fact, in a context of growing social and economic inequality, the problem remains nothing less than knowing if the rights in question only exist on paper or if they can really mean something in practice for those who want to invoke them before the courts. Do they have legally binding value? And thus, how can one develop a coherent legal and institutional framework for adjudicating these rights as justiciable ones? Instead of framing the question of justiciability around problematic attempts at distinguishing economic and social rights from civil and political ones and assessing the role of court in relation to these two categories of rights, it would be more fruitful to rethink the issue of justiciability from the very standpoint of the rights holders themselves—which requires a paradigm shift in the approach to such an issue.

Overview of comparative experiences of justiciability: A growing body of jurisprudence

Adjudication of economic and social rights is already put into practice, to varying degrees, in many courts throughout the world. Several courts and judges have adjudicated a wide variety of these rights, including labor-related rights, the right to health, the right to housing, and the right to food. One cannot ignore the growing body of jurisprudence coming from high level domestic courts and regional and international human rights courts or monitoring bodies that have adjudicated these rights. Knowing that both judicial decisions (i.e. decisions of domestic and international courts) and quasi-judicial decisions (such as UN treaty bodies) have come into play, this ongoing practical process of adjudication by various courts around the world demonstrates that economic and social rights can constitute the basis for judging whether a State has conformed with a legal duty.

At an international level, the Optional Protocol to the International Covenant on Economic, Social and Cultural Rights was finally adopted by the United Nations General Assembly on 10 December

2008 and opened for signature on 24 September 2009. This new international treaty establishes complaint and inquiry mechanisms for the International Covenant on Economic, Social and Cultural Rights. As of July 2010, the Protocol has 32 signatories and 2 parties. It will enter into force when ratified by 10 parties. But the Committee on Economic, Social and Cultural Rights[10] has already made remarkable efforts to insert the perspective of rights claiming constituencies into its "jurisprudence", focusing on vulnerable groups in its assessment of state obligations to respect, protect and fulfill. In particular, its General Comment No. 9,[11] adopted in 1998, strongly reminds us of the principle that a rights holder of *any* human right must have access to an effective remedy, which is affirmed in article 8 of the Universal Declaration of Human Rights in relation to *all* human rights; and underlines that institutional roles or limitations determined by states must be assigned in a manner which implements this principle of a right to an effective remedy for economic and social rights.

But significant progress has also been realized at the domestic and regional levels in the adjudication of social and economic rights. These rights claims are now considered by regional bodies (such as the African Commission on Human Rights, the Inter-American Commission of Human Rights, the Inter-American Court of Human Rights, the European Committee of Social Rights and the European Court of Human Rights). In addition, increasing numbers of domestic constitutions include economic and social rights as justiciable rights. India and South Africa are the most well-known examples; but good practices and creative case law have developed in other countries too. Even where economic and social rights are not directly incorporated into domestic law, all decision-making—whether in courts or in administrative bodies—must be exercised consistently with the *International Covenant on Economic, Social and Cultural Rights*: in other words, domestic law must be interpreted and applied so as to provide, wherever possible, effective remedies to these rights.

As a result, any serious international and comparative survey of relevant jurisprudence makes it difficult to sustain either the argument that economic and social rights lack the qualities of justiciability or the contention that only "some" aspects of such rights are or might be inherently justiciable.[12] Indeed, a surprising number of cases from a variety of legal systems allows us to assess not only if the courts have been willing to address the issue and had the courage to be creative, but also if they have been able to deal effectively with the adjudication of social rights.

Courts have diverse ways of dealing with social and economic rights, or even aspects of them. Brought before the judge, such rights have firstly been litigated directly; in these cases, judgments are made expressly on the basis of social and economic rights. In other cases, it happened that social and economic rights were derived from civil and political ones[13]—which confirmed the interrelationship and indivisibility of these rights. Finally, it appeared that—since some rights may be classified as either civil and political or social and economic in nature—such rights may be used by litigants and judges to give effect to social and economic interests.[14]

When adjudicating, courts are necessarily addressing these government obligations which are related to social and economic rights, i.e. the duties to respect, protect and fulfill. As to the first duty, particularly cases concerning forced evictions[15]—which constitute violations of the obligation to respect the right of housing—provide evidence of the granting of procedural and increasingly substantive protection against State interference and the rigorous way some courts apply human rights norms to evictions.[16] As to the duty to protect, judicial scrutiny has also been attracted to governments failing to take steps to prevent violations by private actors and establish the requisite regulatory mechanisms and laws.[17] Concerning the duty for states to fulfill economic and social rights, there are a number of different ways to adjudicate. We will focus here more precisely on the judicial application of equality norms with regard to states' positive obligations to address the needs of disadvantaged groups.

Of central importance to the adjudication of social and economic rights is their relationship with the right to equality and non-discrimination. In fact, most violations of social and economic rights are directly linked to systemic inequalities. Importantly, reference to social and economic rights may help courts to move beyond a mere formal or procedural (and thus narrow) notion of non-discrimination and turn in a more decisive way to substantive or concrete equality. It may sound difficult to include "poverty" or "social and economic status" within the traditional conceptualization of discrimination. However, nothing prevents courts from making that link.[18]

Finally, as famously discussed in the *Grootboom* case by the South African Constitutional Court,[19] governments' obligations to fulfill social and economic rights includes an obligation to develop a plan to progressively realize such rights. A significant number of jurisprudential cases deal with this obligation to take concrete steps towards realizing economic rights. But approaches may differ: while some courts underline the necessity of achieving an immediate minimum level of realization,[20] others favor the obligation to progressively realize a right in relation to available resources and may also be secured into longer term orders issued by the judge.

Are the rights of the poor, poor rights? The long way to justiciability in France

Social rights of constitutional value can be invoked before the court, either to guide the judge's interpretation of any legal provision or to challenge the legality of administrative regulations or of acts of private law before the competent jurisdiction. But French scholars are generally still reluctant to recognize social rights' justiciability (which, distinct from their invocability, implies a *direct effect*). According to the dominant legal school of thought, positive social rights are not justiciable in the traditional meaning of the term: since they do not embody "subjective rights", private parties cannot directly rely on them before the ordinary judge to claim access to particular benefits or services from public authorities; to have direct effects, such rights need some legislative consolidation. However, according to other eminent scholars, positive social rights do have a "normative justiciability" and it is possible for judges to set aside or nullify norms undermining the implementation of these rights (see Braibant 2001: 46). A brief overview of case law—characterized by judges' tendency of self-restraint—will help us to understand how difficult the recognition of social rights judiciability is in France.

A brief overview of constitutional jurisprudence

The ongoing constitutionalization of social rights

Although since the Constitutional Court's ruling of 1971 the legally binding character of social rights has been well established, in practice the impact of such "constitutionalization" appears limited in a sense. In France, as elsewhere, discussions concerning social rights as justiciable rights often tend to be polemical. And there, too, there are different degrees of judicial scrutiny and the scope of judicial review may be limited: if the Constitutional Council strictly controls any law involving "*droits-libertés*", it allows the Parliament and the Government an important margin of appreciation when positive social rights are concerned. A brief overview of the constitutional jurisprudence shows how much this scope of judicial review is limited and indicates that two scenarios have been envisaged by the Constitutional Council.

In the first one, the constitutional court mentions positive social rights (for example, the right to employment[21] or the right to health[22]) to justify legislative action. In this case, however, the social rights guaranteed by the 1946 Preamble survive as a constitutional review only if, as implemented by Parliament, they do not undermine other fundamental rights disproportionately. From this case law, it becomes evident that the 1946 Preamble can be relied upon by the legislature to validate, in conformity with the Constitution, public policies in the social field—even if in so doing it may limit the exercise of other competing fundamental rights. However, the Constitutional Council does not allow for such limitations to substantially affect their exercise.

In the second scenario, social rights serve as constitutional arguments to invalidate legislation each time their scope appears to be restricted. In other words, to be validated as conforming to the Constitution, the legislation should not deprive the pertinent fundamental social right of sufficient "legal guarantees",[23] they should not, in other words, annihilate its effectiveness. This having been said, the Constitutional Council—which has so far avoided defining the minimum contents of social rights—affords the Parliament a wide margin of interpretation.

French courts and the justiciability of human rights guaranteed by international instruments

How can French courts admit the justiciability of human rights guaranteed by international instruments? Since space is too limited here to answer in detail, we will focus on an important judgment delivered by the *Cour de cassation* in May 2005, regarding the New York Convention on the Rights of the Child of 26 January 1990. It is, in fact, the first time that the Court has recognized the "direct applicability" of Article 3-1 (*"In all actions concerning children, whether undertaken by public or private social welfare institutions, courts of law, administrative authorities or legislative bodies, the best interests of the child shall be a primary consideration"*) and Article 12.2 (*"For this purpose, the child shall in particular be provided the opportunity to be heard in any judicial and administrative proceedings affecting the child, either directly, or through a representative or an appropriate body, in a manner consistent with the procedural rules of national law"*) of the Convention.[24] This judgment is important in that such provisions—understood as exclusively conferring obligations on the

State—were previously denied justiciability. Thanks to this, the case law of the *Cour de cassation* is now finally in line with the approach adopted by the *Conseil d'État* (the French administrative supreme court), which has been the first to accept the justiciability of certain provisions of the New York Convention (see Abraham 1998: 15).

The special case of the right to decent housing: Enshrined in the legislation and enforceable

The "right" to decent housing is a particularly interesting case concerning the problem of justiciability. In several European countries, there is current debate on the notion of a "justiciable right to housing" and a number of courts around the world have already given effect to the principle of duties of immediate effect. Over and above the recognition in legislation and regulations, the justiciable right to housing involves conferring on authorities not only the obligation of providing the means to facilitate access to quality housing, but also of results. By establishing an enforceable right to housing, such justiciability allows citizens to gain access to a court to take action against authorities responsible for having failed to provide decent, stable housing. In France, although a justiciable right to housing has been recognized, its implementation remains difficult.

Very active with litigation on the judicial front, several associations have tried to convince courts of the necessity of making the right to decent housing directly enforceable against reluctant authorities or private parties. The right to adequate housing was first recognized in France in the Besson Act of 31 May 1990 and has been qualified by the Constitutional Council as a goal with constitutional status, yet many deplored the incomplete character of such a legal protection which does not allow for any redress before the courts in cases in which this right has not been respected. Given the catastrophic situation,[25] a national debate on the necessity of recognizing the legal right to adequate housing in a new law that could stand up in court was conducted in 2007. Introduced at a time when homelessness was seen to be a growing and unacceptable social problem, a new law on the legal right to housing was passed as an emergency measure in March 2007.[26] The enforceable right to housing (DALO) Act, establishing the justiciable right to housing as well as other social cohesion measures, came into force on 1 January 2008. It recognized the right to decent, independent housing to all persons legally residing on French territory (French citizens and others lawfully living in France) who were not able to obtain this by their own means and resources. This new law also provides for access to the courts for victims in cases of violation of its provisions and creates an oversight committee to monitor the implementation of this right. In other words, the justiciable right to housing introduced in France replaces public authorities' "best-effort" obligation with a performance obligation whereby certain categories of social housing applicants are entitled to apply for legal relief if they have been waiting for housing for "an abnormally long time".[27]

Concretely, and generally with the help of a social worker, someone can appeal if they face one of three situations: they have applied for social housing and have not been offered suitable housing after an abnormally long time (which is fixed by the prefect and differs from one department to another); they are either unhoused (homeless or staying with someone), under threat of eviction with no possibility of rehousing, living in a hostel for more than six months or temporarily living in move-on housing for more than eighteen months, living in premises not meant for habitation, substandard or dangerous, or living in overcrowded or indecent premises (because of having a child or disabled dependent, or being themselves disabled); they have applied for a place in temporary accommodation but have been made no appropriate offer in reply to their application. Since 1 January 2008, mediation committees established in each department can help to reach a negotiated settlement: if they have no power to (re)house, these committees have to notify the prefect of the department within three months (or six months in the larger departments) of the households that are considered priority cases along with a recommendation letter of how their housing needs should be met. The mediation committee decisions themselves can be challenged through the ordinary procedures in the administrative court in the same way as any administrative decision. And households which have not been offered housing within three or six months of the committee's decision are entitled to file an "appeal for judicial review" to the administrative court which must give an emergency ruling within two months and can then order the government to (re)house the applicant from the prefectoral quota.

Although promising, the new law has been strongly criticized by civil society and vehemently debated in academic circles. While, according to the NGOs, it protects only those persons who are legally resident in France (excluding de facto significant numbers of persons without formal residency status, like the homeless), several constitutional law experts denounced the law as complicated and as having the illusory character of a right existing in practice for adequate housing. The next few years will show if the law produces an improvement in the situation of rights holders. As underlined by the Haut Comité pour le Logement des Personnes Défavorisées, the prefectoral quota is not sufficient to satisfy all priority applications and the implementation of the justiciable right to housing will demand a substantial increase in the housing budget. Ten months after the Act was introduced, some 50,000 appeals have been lodged, far less than the 80,000 to 100,000 expected. The Fondation Abbé Pierre explains the low number of appeals by the fact that potential applicants are not fully informed. To improve the information meant for people eligible for the DALO, Secours Catholique and Fondation Abbé Pierre set up a mobile outreach team (the "DALO bus") to promote the justiciable right in different towns across France. But the lack of information is not the only explanatory factor. The appeal procedures are very complex and lodging an appeal is likely to be difficult for many potential applicants. It remains that, despite such difficulties and challenges, this enforceable rights-based approach helped to overcome the invisibility around those suffering housing deprivation.

Concluding remarks on the need for research in action: From knowledge to legal strategies

Justiciability is not the only means of enforcing social rights. The full realization of these rights depends primarily on action by the executive and legislative branches of the State. However, denying judicial intervention in this field has serious negative impact, reducing the remedies victims of social rights violations can claim. At the same time, it weakens the accountability of the State and may foster impunity for violations. Keeping this in mind helps us to understand the importance of the various academic initiatives taken to convey a better sense of how the adjudication of social and economic rights operates in practice.

As the academic debate about judicial enforcement of social rights is undergoing changes, research oriented initiatives have in fact an important role to play to inform both practice and theory. Comparative domestic case law concerning social rights provides a useful source of law and tools to promote the expansion of justiciability; in the same way, analyzing international and regional experiences can offer valuable arguments to help overcome prejudices in those jurisdictions where some limitations still exist. In the past few years such initiatives to learn about and discuss the judicial answerability of social and economic rights have tended to increase in number in various countries and regions. Trying to rethink the universality as well as the indivisibility of human rights, such initiatives are also very often, if not always, pursuing advocacy purposes. This is, for example, the case of the recently launched International Network for Economic, Social and Cultural Rights (ESCR-Net),[28] which is a collaborative project that compiles and analyses paradigmatic jurisprudence and other decisions from national courts and international human rights bodies related to economic, social and cultural rights; the goal here is to encourage discussion of crucial challenges for advocacy and the use of legal strategies as valid and effective means for claiming economic, social and cultural rights.

In France, the research program entitled "Droits des pauvres, pauvres droits? Recherche sur la justiciabilité des droits sociaux"[29] (The Rights of the Poor, Poor Rights? Research Program on the Justiciability of Social Rights) and hosted by Paris X-Nanterre University aims at scrutinizing both the academic debate and the jurisdictional answers concerning the nature and regime of social rights. More precisely, it focuses on two special research fields: the juridical and political issues in the legal theories concerning the opposition between civil and political rights on the one hand, and economic and social rights on the other; the social rights' regime chosen by the judges. Questioning the way in which courts and other bodies address the issues that have been raised with regard to the justiciability of these rights, this research program provides an overview and an analysis of the diverse jurisdictional arguments: the arguments of French but also of foreign judges, European judges (the European Court of Human Rights and the European Court of Justice), international judges (the African Court, the Inter-American Court), as well as of quasi-judicial bodies (the European Committee of Social Rights, the Committee on Economic, Social and Cultural Rights) are examined. It is clearly in order to understand their different judicial answers when dealing with social claims that the research program addresses the question of the justiciability of social and economic rights. Far from being understood narrowly, judicial decisions are analyzed in their context, in relation to other actors of case law, not only the parties themselves but also the academic research (doctrine) and the practitioners contributing to the judicial response. If, quite classically, this research first consists of setting out and analyzing case law and legal research literature, it also aims—and this is its originality—to list, in various countries, the lawyers who specialize in fundamental rights in order to make direct interviews on the justiciability of social rights a specific issue.[30] Importantly, this research—based on an internationalist and comparative approach—also sheds light on both national/regional diversity and converging evolutions which characterize the social rights issue: since economic and social rights jurisprudence and scholarship have shown a tendency for a long time to over-emphasize criteria for identifying violations to be applied universally without reference to the historical circumstances that could only be considered in the context of particular claims, such an approach has its importance. Here too, and finally, the purpose is to analyze the use of Law and rights as instruments of political action in the fight against poverty: helping to clarify the situation in France, such a research program ultimately offers suggestions for adjustments to the law.

Notes

Preface

1 This book stems from a symposium co-organized at Nichifutsukaikan (Maison Franco Japonaise) on this theme in Tokyo in 2009. The co-organizers were the Global COE Program Center for the Study of Social Stratification and Inequality at Tohoku University, Sendai and the French Research Institute on Contemporary Japan (UMIFRE n°19 MAEE CNRS) at Nichifutsukaikan, Tokyo. The papers selected from this symposium have been revised by their authors to contribute to the project of this book.

Chapter 2

* This is a reproduction of Sato (2010) with the permission of De Gruyter, the publisher of *Contemporary Japan*. I gratefully thank the publisher for their permission.

1 Nippon Keidanren, a major organization of employers in Japan, proposed three types of workers in 1995. These were (1) workers who accumulate skills without fixed-term employment contracts, (2) workers who have specialized skills with fixed-term employment contracts, and (3) flexible workers with fixed-term employment contracts. Even though Nippon Keidanren promotes the second and third types of workers to reduce labor costs and to increase flexibility in employment, it still acknowledges the importance of the first type of workers.

2 Although intergenerational mobility is an important topic in the study of social stratification and social mobility, we do not deal with it in this paper. This is because mobility table analysis does not capture the exact timing when respondents obtained their current jobs and, therefore, contains little information on the current situation of social stratification in Japan. Nevertheless, Ishida's (2008) event history analysis of the subject shows that the likelihood of a person in their mid-career to be a professional or a manager if a parent is also a professional or manager has recently become stronger even after controlling for the effect of education. This finding reveals the stability of the upper strata of professionals and managers.

3 NEETs are young people who are Not in Employment, Education, or Training.

4 See also Hashimoto (2007) for the possible emergence of "a new class society."

Chapter 4

1 The lost decade in Japan refers to the period from 1992 to 2002 when Japan suffered a prolonged recession.

Chapter 5

1 Which can also be called "working conditions" in the wider sense of the term.
2 Which can also be called "job conditions" in the wider sense of the term.
3 Throughout the rest of this article, the authors will use the terms "constraint" or "constraining factor" in this sense only.

Chapter 7

1 The Universal Declaration of Human Rights identifies numerous rights that are not opposable, even by states if they are signatories to this declaration. For example, Article 23 reads: "everyone, without any discrimination, has the right to equal pay for equal work." But although this right is not opposable, women everywhere are paid less than men for equal work and cannot get their right to equal pay enforced.

Chapter 8

1 Inaba Tsuyoshi was a member of the Inoken and participated in the mobilization of homeless people from the start. He became one of the leaders of the Coalition of Shinjuku in 1995. He is still a major figure of the Coalition, sharing its activity with another NPO called 'Moyai' which he co-founded in 1998. The purpose of Moyai is to support homeless people's access to housing.

Chapter 9

1 Many of the homeless at the time were male construction laborers who had lost their jobs during the recession after supporting Japan's rapid economic growth. One movement led by the day laborers' union was organized in the eastern district of Tokyo and the other movement was formed mainly by men in the services and other new urban sundry industries who had lost their jobs.
2 The following is a list of events that directly involved Japanese and French anti-poverty movements (event locations in brackets.)
    1999 AC! Activists visited Japan (Tokyo).
    2000 The Caravan of Have-nots to the Summit in Okinawa (Tokyo, Nagoya, Osaka and Naha).
    2000 Japanese activists visited Paris (Paris).
    2001 AC! Activists visited Japan (Tokyo).
    2002 The World Social Forum (Porto Alegre).
    2003 The International Solidarity of Have-nots was launched (the European Social Forum).
    2003 The European Social Forum (Paris).
    2004 Participation in the NoVox rally at the World Social Forum (Mumbai).
    2004 The European Social Forum (London).
    2005 Protests against the government's response to urban riots in France (Tokyo).
    2005 The World Social Forum (Porto Alegre).

2006 DAL occupied Japan Tourism Office in protest against forced removal of the homeless from Osaka Utsubo Park (Paris).
2006 DAL activists visited Japan (Tokyo and Osaka).
2007 DAL activists visited Japan (Tokyo, Osaka and Nagoya).
2007 DAL occupied the French headquarters at the World Championships in Athletics in protest against forced removal of the homeless from Osaka Nagai Park.
2007 The World Social Forum (Nairobi).
2007 European Marches against the Summit in Heiligendamm (France–Belgium–Germany).
2007 Protests in front of the French embassy and consulate in solidarity with DAL's action in la rue de la Banque (Tokyo and Osaka).
2008 NoVox activists visited Japan, the Summit in Tōyako (Tokyo, Osaka, Nagoya, Sapporo and Toyoura).
2008 The NoVox International Solidarity Forum (Paris).
2010 The Novox International Solidarity Forum (Tokyo and Osaka).

3 While this is not the subject of this chapter, the meritocracy principle is as pervasive in Japanese society as in French society and the myth of equality through school education has been accepted widely. In fact, the degree to which children's occupations are determined by their parents' occupations is relatively small in Japan among the OECD countries (OECD 2007).

4 The homeless in a literal sense are often socially excluded due to mental or alcohol-induced illnesses to start with, and they are the subjects of charity work by organizations such as Emmaüs. However, they have never been the actors of social movements.

5 Although the participants of the DAL movement are not 'fighting for recognition', the issue concerning one's dignity is important when taking part in the movement. M participates in DAL's activities while dealing with his own housing problem. He says that the biggest reason for him to take active part in the DAL movement is that he was 'treated properly' when he visited DAL for consultation. People in poor living environments experience humiliation on a daily basis even though they know it is not their fault. In addition to the contemptuous looks, the bullying their children suffer, and a feeling of inferiority when their children cannot have their friends around, they have experienced inhumane treatment at government offices.

6 APEIS stands for Association Pour l'Emploi et l'Information et la Solidarité (Association for Employment, Information and Solidarity).

7 The Osaka-based movement tended to fight for livelihood protection through the courts even in the early days, which is an example of seeking state intervention. The Tokyo-based movement subsequently changed its strategy and developed campaigns to seek livelihood protection through welfare benefits.

Chapter 10

1 Other measures, with a more limited scope, had already been introduced in the late 1980s and early 1990s. In 1989, exemptions from employers' social contributions were granted for the hiring of the first employee; in 1991, tax exemptions for the employment of domestic children's nurses were also created.

2 Today, the threshold for exemption from employers' social contributions is 1.6 SMIC (guaranteed minimum wage). Considering the strong concentration of jobs in the lowest part of the wage distribution, this measure concerns more than half (approximately 60 percent) of all jobs.
3 The policy of reducing working hours has been gradually dismantled since 2002. We will not discuss this issue here.
4 The RSA substitutes for the general minimum income guarantee (RMI, *Revenu minimum d'insertion*) and for the specific allowance concerning lone parents (API, *Allocation de parent isolé*).
5 We can underline here a kind of optical illusion considering that social security contributions, because they are paid by the employers, are not part of the employees' compensation.
6 With this law, unemployed people are bound to accept a "reasonable" job offer. The main characteristic of the "reasonable" job offer is the level of the wage, which declines incrementally after 3, 6 and 12 months of unemployment. Workers are thus forced to gradually reduce their wage claims. An unemployed person who refuses two "reasonable" job offers is disqualified and receives no unemployment benefit.
7 The latest change in the definition of underemployment took place in 2009. As a consequence approximately 250,000 persons "disappeared" from the statistics.
8 Moreover, other problems (health, transportation, child care, lack of qualifications, etc) are in many cases much more important than financial incentives to explain the difficulties in getting back to employment.
9 The federal minimum wage in the United States represents around 45 percent of median hourly earnings, compared with a figure of around 55 percent to 60 percent in France.
10 "The Report which I now present is a sequel to my earlier Report, in that it is concerned with what was named in that Report as one of the assumptions of Social Security: the assumption that employment is maintained, and mass unemployment prevented" (Beveridge 1944: 17).

Chapter 11

1 While paragraph 5 stipulates that "each person has the duty to work and the right to employment", paragraph 10 announces that the state "shall provide the individual and the family with the conditions necessary to their development", paragraph 11 protects the right to health and social security (especially in the form of social assistance), paragraph 12 deals with the articulation between social security and equality in times of disaster, and paragraph 13 concerns the right to education.
2 Usually called "*droits-libertés*", the individual rights protected by the founding text of French political modernity are conceived as implying a (political or civic) freedom to act, as well as the principle of inherent limits on state power. Differently speaking, as long as liberty is guaranteed in the constitution, the individual is protected from undue intervention from public authorities. In that sense, the rights protected by the 1789 Declaration are also said to exemplify the decisive legal notion of subjective rights.
3 See for example the strongly critical analysis made by Dany Cohen (1999), "Le droit à..." (The right to...), in *L'avenir du droit. Mélanges en homage à François Terré*, Paris: Dalloz, p. 393.

4 See J. Rivero 1990, "Déclarations parallèles et nouveaux droits de l'homme", *Revue trimestrielle des droits de l'homme*, No. 2, p. 323. For a synthetic presentation of the opinions of two other major figures, Léon Duguit and Maurice Hauriou, see C. de la Mardière (1999), "Retour sur la valeur juridique de la Déclaration de 1789", *Revue française de droit constitutionnel*, No. 38, p. 235.
5 CC, July 16, 1971, No. 71-44 DC.
6 *International Covenant on Civil and Political Rights* and *International Covenant on Economic, Social and Cultural Rights*, both adopted and opened for signature, ratification and accession by General Assembly resolution 2200A (XXI) of 16 December 1966, and entered into force respectively 23 March and 3 January 1976; texts on line: Office of the United Nations High Commissioner for Human Rights (http://www2.ohchr.org/english/law/ccpr.htm and http://www2.ohchr.org/english/law/cescr.htm). While the *International Covenant on Civil and Political Rights* provided for an optional complaints procedure at the time of its adoption, none has been designed for the *International Covenant on Economic, Social and Cultural Rights* during the more than forty years since that time.
7 It is difficult to list here in an exhaustive way all the jurisdictions in which social and economic rights have been deemed justiciable and judicially enforceable; *inter alia*, these include Bangladesh, Columbia, Finland, Kenya, Hungary, Latvia, the Philippines, Switzerland, Venezuela, South Africa, Ireland, India, Argentina and the USA. For more details, see A. Nolan et al., "Leading Cases on Economic, Social and Cultural Rights: Summaries—Working Paper No.2" (Geneva; COHRE, 2005), available at www.cohre.org.
8 These include the African Commission on Human Rights, the Inter-American Commission of Human Rights, the Inter-American Court of Human Rights, the European Committee of Social Rights, and the European Court of Human Rights. For a list of decisions of regional bodies related to social and economic rights, see *ibid.*
9 *Draft Optional Protocol to the International Covenant on Economic, Social and Cultural Rights*, Human Rights Council, Sixth Session, Open-ended Working Group on an Optional Protocol to the International Covenant on Economic, Social and Cultural Rights, Fourth session Geneva, 16–27 July 2007 A/HRC/6/WG.4/2 (23 April 2007).
10 http://www2.ohchr.org/english/bodies/cescr/
11 Committee on Economic, Social and Cultural Rights, General Comment No.9, *The Domestic Application of the Covenant*, 3 December 1998, E/C.12/1998/24, CESCR.
12 For international and comparative reviews of case law, see for example: Squires et al., 2005 and Langford 2009.
13 In this sense, the Indian courts have understood the right to life to "take within its sweep" the right to food, the right to clothing, the right to decent environment and a reasonable accommodation to live in; see *Shantistar Builders v. Narayan Khimatal Tomtame*, Supreme Court of India, Civil Appeal No. 2598/1989, 31 January 1990.
14 For example, the Human Rights Committee has emphasized that the right to equality/non-discrimination provided for in Article 26 of the International Covenant on Civil and Political Rights applies to the enjoyment of social and economic rights, including social security benefits.

15 In this sense and for example, the South African Constitutional Court in the case *Port Elizabeth Municipality* affirmed 'the need for special judicial control' of the process of eviction: even if there is no constitutional requirement for the state to provide housing to any evicted household, "a court should be reluctant to grant an eviction against relatively settled occupiers unless it is satisfied that a reasonable alternative is available"; *Port Elizabeth Municipality v. Various Occupiers* (1) 2005 SA 217 (CC), paragraphs 18 and 28.
16 Evictions cases are not the only concerned; a similar evolution from procedural to substantive protections has occurred in many other areas, such as in cases concerning disconnections of water supplies (Argentina, Brazil, and South-Africa), social security (Russia), denial of access to health and education (Columbia).
17 For example, the European Court of Human Rights has criticized governments for failing to protect rights to the home, family and private life by not regulating industrial pollution adequately; see *Lopez Ostra v. Spain* (1994) IIHRL 106 (December 1994).
18 In this sense, a decision of the Ontario Board of Inquiry (1998) further upheld by the Division Court (2001) made clear that, due to the strong correlation between poverty and membership in groups protected from discrimination, denials of housing on the ground of poverty or low income level constitute discrimination on a number of grounds (including race, sex, marital status, age, citizenship status and receipt of public assistance) (see Porter 2004: 133).
19 According to the Court, government authorities had failed to develop appropriate housing programs related to emergency relief for those without access to basic shelter, thereby violating their duty to take reasonable legislative and other measures to progressively realize the constitutional right to have access to adequate housing; *South Africa v. Grootboom*, 2001 (1) SA 46 (CC).
20 Interestingly, even in the UK—traditionally hostile to social and economic rights—the House of Lords recognized that "it is well arguable that human rights include the right to a minimum standard of living, without which many of the other rights would be a mockery"; *Matthews v. Ministry of Defence* (2003) UKHL 4, paragraph 26.
21 As was the case when, in a highly controversial context, the Constitutional Council ruled in 2000 that the legislation reducing the legal length of the working week to 35 hours merely implemented paragraphs 5 and 11 of the 1946 Preamble; CC, January 13, 2000, No. 99-423 DC.
22 In 1991, the Constitutional Council declared that measures prohibiting or restricting advertisements in favor of tobacco and alcohol are aimed at guaranteeing for all the protection of health in conformity with paragraph 11 of the 1946 Preamble; CC, January 8, 1991, No. 90-283 DC, paragraph 8.
23 CC, August 14, 2003, No. 2003-483 DC, paragraph 8.
24 Cass. 1er civ., 18 May 2005, Bull. No. 212, reaffirmed in Cass. 1er civ., 14 June 2005, Bull No. 245.
25 From 1990 to 2006, the situation dramatically deteriorated. In 2007, the Abbé Pierre Foundation denounced the apathy of the government in the face of increasing numbers of forced evictions, the inadequate character of about three million persons' housing, and the nearly 900,000 housing units lacking relative to overall needs (Bissuel 2006; Meunier 2006).

26 *Loi n. 2007-290 du 5 mars 2007 instituant le droit au logement opposable et portant diverses mesures en faveur de la cohésion sociale* (http://www.legifrance.gouv.fr/affichTexte.do?cidTexte=JORFTEXT000000271094&dateTexte=)
27 This law is very progressive: it provides for phases allowing a first priority category of the population (the persons with the most pressing needs) to be able to go to court in case of violation of the right to housing as of 1 December 2008; and a second category of persons being allowed to do so from January 2012.
28 http://www.escr-net.org/
29 http://droits-sociaux.u-paris10.fr/
30 Some international human rights lawyers are associated to the project; see, for an example among the listed useful links, the web site of Claire Mahon http://www.clairemahon.net/

Bibliography

Abraham, R. (1998), "La notion d'effet direct des traités internationaux devant le Conseil d'État (à propos de la Convention de New York sur les droits de l'enfant)," *Recueil Dalloz*, jurisprudence, p. 15.
Afsa, C. (2008), "Estimer la valeur monétaire de la qualité d'un emploi. L'exemple des salariés en fin de carrière," *Revue Économique*, 59(3): 59.
Agata, K. (2008), "Shokureki keisei ni okeru shikaku riyōsha no bunseki (An analysis of utilizing vocational qualifications in career formation)," in K. Agata (ed.), *Hatarakikata to kyaria keisei (2005-nen SSM chōsa shirīzu 4)* (Work style and career formation (The 2005 SSM research series; 4)), 85–102. Sendai: The 2005 SSM Research Committee.
Aizawa, S. and S. Miwa (2008), "2005-nen SSM dēta ni okeru keizaiteki fu-byōdō shihyō no kisoteki kentō: Setai shūnyū ochūsin ni (Economic inequality of Japanese society: Trends in income distribution in two recent decades)," in S. Miwa and D. Kobayashi (eds), *2005-nen SSM Nihon chōsa no kiso bunseki: Kōzō-sūsei-hōhō (2005-nen SSM chōsa shirīzu 1)* (Basic analysis of the 2005 SSM survey in Japan (The 2005 SSM research series; 1)), 95–109. Sendai: The 2005 SSM Research Committee.
Aliaga, C., B. Duplouy and S. Jugnot (2010) "Enquête Génération 2004, Méthodologie et Bilan," *Net.Doc*, 63(148): 5–608.
Anker, R. et al. (2003), "La mesure du travail décent: un système d'indicateurs statistiques de l'OIT," *Revue Internationale du Travail*, 142(2): 365–395.
Atkinson, A. B. (1983), *Social justice and public policy*, Brighton: Wheatsheaf.
Atkinson, A. B. and G. V. Mogensen (1993), *Welfare and work incentives: A North European perspective*, New-York: Clarendon.
Aubin, E. (2008), *Droit de l'aide et de l'action sociales*, Paris: Lextenso.
Avenell, S. (2009), "Civil Society and the New Civic Movements in Contemporary Japan: Convergence, Collaboration, and Transformation," *Journal of Japanese Studies* 35(2): 247–283.
Baudelot C. and R. Establet (2009), *L'élitisme républicain: l'école française à l'épreuve des comparaisons internationales*, Paris: Le Seuil.
Belleville-Pla, A. (2004), "Les trajectoires professionnelles des bénéficiaires de minima sociaux," DREES, *Études et Résultats*, 320, juin.
Bescond D., A. Châtaigner and F. Mehran (2003), "Sept indicateurs pour mesurer le travail décent: une comparaison internationale," *Revue internationale du travail*, 142(2): 195–229.
Beveridge, W. H. (1944), *Full employment in a free society*, London: George Allen & Unwin.
Bissuel, B. (2006), "Droit au logement: un mirage pour les pauvres?," *Le Monde*, 31 Août.
Borgetto, M. (2007), "Le Conseil constitutionnel, le principe d'égalité et les droits sociaux," *Billets d'humeur dédiés à D. Lochak*, Paris: L.G.D.J.
Boucobza, I., T. Gründler, M. Pichard, and D. Roman (2010), "Les droits sociaux dans le discours de la doctrine française: Entre relégation et

réception," *Actes du Colloque international d'Istanbul sur les droits sociaux* (15–16 octobre 2009); see also: http://droits-sociaux.u-paris10.fr/assets/files/conferences/CRistanbul.pdf

Braibant, G. (2001), *La Charte des droits fondamentaux de l'Union européenne*, Paris: Éditions du Seuil.

Brinton, M. C. (2008), "After the bubble: Young men's labor market entry experiences in the 1990s and beyond," in H. Tarohmaru (ed.), *Jakunensō no shakai idō to kaisōka (2005-nen SSM chōsa shirīzu 11)* (Social stratification and social mobility of young Japanese (The 2005 SSM research series; 11)), 13–35. Sendai: The 2005 SSM Research Committee.

CAS (2007), "Jeunes Français, jeunes Allemands: regards croisés sur les premiers pas dans la vie professionnelle," *Notes de Veille*, 26 février, 47.

Cazes C. and N. Missègue (2001), "Une forte segmentation des emplois dans les activités de services," *Économie et Statistiques*, 344: 81–108.

CERC (2008), *Un devoir national—L'insertion des jeunes sans diplôme*, rapport n°9, Paris: La Documentation française.

Chabanet, D. and J. Faniel (2007), "L'Europe du chômage: enjeux et dynamiques socio-politiques d'un échec," *Politique Européenne*, 21: 5–19.

Chauvel, L. (2006), "Les nouvelles générations devant la panne prolongée de l'ascenseur social," *Revue de l'OFCE*, 35–51.

Cheyron, P. du and D. Gélot (eds) (2007), *Droit et Pauvreté*, Contributions issues du séminaire ONPES/DREES/MiRe.

Cloutier, L. (2009), "Évolution de la qualité de l'emploi des femmes et des hommes au Québec entre 1997 et 2007," thèse de Sciences humaines appliquées, Université de Montréal.

Cohen, D. (1999), "Le droit à…" (The right to…), in *L'avenir du droit. Mélanges en hommage à François Terré*, Paris: Dalloz, 393–400.

Concialdi, P. and S. Ponthieux (2000), "Low pay and poor workers: A comparative study of France and the USA," *Transfer*, 6: 650–672, Winter.

Coomans, F. (ed.) (2006), *Justiciability of Economic and Social Rights*, Maastricht: Intersentia, Maastricht Series in Human Rights.

Daniel, C. (1998), "Les politiques d'emploi: une révolution silencieuse," *Droit Social*, 1: 3–11, janvier.

Davis, K. and W. E. Moore (1945), "Some principles of stratification," *American Sociological Review*, 10(2): 242–249.

Davoine, L. and Ehrel, C. (2006), "La qualité de l'emploi: une mise en perspective européenne," in CEE, *La Qualité de l'Emploi*, Coll. Repères, Paris: La Découverte.

Devetter, F.-X. (2002), "Vers une nouvelle norme des temps de travail? Temps subis ou temps choisis?" *Formation Emploi*, 78: 53–67.

Devetter, F.-X. (2009), "Gender differences in time availability: Professional logics beyond the impact of domestic sphere," *Gender, Work and Organization*, 16(4): 429–450.

Dubet, F. (2004), *Les inégalités multiples*, Paris: Seuil (Edition de poche).

Dubet, F. (2009), *Le travail des sociétés*, Paris: Seuil.

Durand, C. (2005), "Le mouvement altermondialiste: de nouvelle pratiques organisationnelles pour l'émancipation," *Mouvements*, 42:103–14.

Durkheim, É. (2007[/1893]), *De la division du travail social*, Paris: PUF, 1930, nouvelle édition "Quadrige".
Durkheim, É. (2007[/1897]), *Le Suicide. Étude de sociologie*, Paris: PUF, nouvelle édition "Quadrige".
Fondeur. Y. and C. Minni (2006), "L'accès des jeunes à l'emploi," *Données sociales—La société française*, 13–21.
Gallie. D. and S. Paugam (eds) (2000), *Welfare regimes and the experience of unemployment in Europe*, Oxford, Oxford University Press.
Genda, Y (2003), "Dangers facing businessmen in their 20s and 30s who work for large companies," *Japan Labor Bulletin*, 42(2): 7–11.
Genda, Y. (2005), *A Nagging Sense of Job Insecurity: The New Reality Facing Japanese Youth*, Tokyo: LTCB International Library Trust, International House of Japan.
Genda, Y. (2007), "Jobless youths and the NEET problem in Japan," *Social Science Japan Journal*, 10(1): 23–40.
Genda, Y. and M. Kurosawa (2001), "Transition from school to work in Japan," *Journal of the Japanese and International Economies*, 15: 465–488.
Genda, Y. and R. Kambayashi (2002), "Declining self-employment in Japan," *Journal of the Japanese and International Economies*, 16: 73–91.
Genda, Y., A. Kondo and S. Ohta (2008), "The endless Ice Age: A review of the cohort effect in Japan," *The Japanese Economy*, 35(3): 55–86.
Genda, Y., A. Kondo and S. Ohta (2010), "Long-term effects of a recession at labor market entry in Japan and the United States," *Journal of Human Resources*, 45(1): 157–196.
Ghai, D. (2003), "Travail décent: concept et indicateurs," *Revue internationale du travail*, 142(2): 121–157
Givord, P. and L. Wilner (2009), "Les contrats temporaires: trappe ou marchepied vers l'emploi stable?," INSEE, *Documents de travail*, G 2009/04.
Gollac, M. and S. Volkoff (2005), *Les conditions de travail*, Coll. Repère, Paris: La Découverte.
Graeber, D. (2002), "The new anarchists," *New Left Review*, 13 Jan–Feb, 61–73.
Graeber, D. (2004), *Fragments of an Anarchist Anthropology*, Chicago: Prickly Paradigm Press.
Granovetter, M. (1995), *Getting a Job*, second edition, Chicago: Chicago University Press.
Greewe, C. and F. Benoit-Rohmer (2003), *Les droits sociaux ou la démolition de quelques poncifs*, Strasbourg: Presses universitaires de Strasbourg.
Grusky, D. B., K. A. Weeden and M. Di Carlo (2008), "The scary takeoff: Why standard accounts of the rise in inequality are wrong (and why we should wish they were right)," Palo Alto: Stanford University, Center for the Study of Poverty and Inequality working paper.
Guillemot, D., P. Pétour and H. Zajdela (2002), "Trappe à chômage ou trappe à pauvreté: quel est le sort des allocataires du RMI?," *Revue économique*, 2002, 53(6): 1235–1252.
Hara, J. and K. Seiyama (2005), *Inequality amid affluence: Social stratification in Japan*, Melbourne: Trans Pacific Press.

Hasegawa, K. and M. Takashi (2009), "Shakai undō to shakai undō ron no gendai (Situation of social movement and social movement theory)," in S. Soranaka, K. Hasegawa, T. Machimura and N. Higuchi (eds), *Shakai undō toiu kōkyō kūkan* (Social movement as shared space), Tokyo: Seibundō.

Hasegawa, M. (2006), *"We are not Garbage," The Homeless Movement in Tokyo, 1994–2002*, New York: Routledge.

Hashimoto, K. (2007), *Atarashii kaikyūshakai atarashii kaikyūtōsō: "Kakusa" de sumasarenai genjitsu* (New class society and new class struggle), Tokyo: Kōbunsha.

Haut Comité pour le Logement des Personnes Défavorisées (2008), *Assumer l'obligation de résultat du droit au logement sur l'ensemble du territoire*, Paris, La Documentation française.

Hayashi, Y. (2008), "Rōdōshijō no ryūdōka to sedainaiidō no kiketsu: Tenshoku ni tomonau chingin henka kōzō no jidaiteki henka (Fluidization of the labor market and consequence of intra-generational mobility: Longitudinal trends on wage changes in job changes)," *Shakaigaku Nenpō* (Annual Reports of the Tohoku Sociological Society), 37: 59–70.

Hirata, S. (2008), "Hiseiki koyō no zōka to kakusa no kakudai: Ryūdōka to tayōka wa hontō ka (Increase of non-standard employment and the enlarging social divide)," in Y. Sato (ed.), *Ryūdōsei to kakusa no kaisōron (2005-nen SSM chōsa shirīzu 15)* (Disparities, social fluidity, and social stratification (The 2005 SSM research series; 15)), 133–152, Sendai: The 2005 SSM Research Committee.

Holloway, J. (2002), *Change the World Without Taking Power: The Meaning of Revolution Today*, London: Pluto.

Honda, Y. (2005), "'Freeters': Young atypical workers in Japan," *Japan Labor Review*, 2(3): 5–25.

Honda, Y., A. Naito and K. Gotoh (2006), *'NEET'tte Iuna!* (Don't Say 'NEET'!), Tokyo: Kobunsha.

Honda, Y. (2005), *Wakamono to shigoto: "Gakkō keiyu no shūshoku" o koete* (Young people and employment in Japan: Beyond the "School-mediated Job Search"), Tokyo: Tokyo Daigaku Shuppankai.

Husson, M. (2002), "Réduction du temps de travail et emploi: une nouvelle évaluation," *La Revue de l'IRES* 38/1: 79–108.

Imai, J. and Y. Sato (2011), "Regular and non-regular employment as an additional duality in Japanese labor market: Institutional perspective on career mobility," in Y. Sato and J. Imai (eds), *Changes in the Japanese welfare-employment regime and inequality*, 1–31, Melbourne: Trans Pacific Press.

Imbert, P.-H. (1989), "Droits des pauvres, pauvre(s) droit(s)? Réflexions sur les droits économiques et sociaux," *RDP* 739–754.

Inada, M. (2008), Chōki koyō no suii: Posuto kōdo keizai seichōki sedai to "shūsin koyō" (A study on the transition of long-term employment in post rapid economic growth Japan)," in H. Takada (ed.), *Kaisō-kaikyū kōzō to chii tassei (2005-nen SSM chōsa shirīzu 2)* (Class structure and status attainment (The 2005 SSM research series; 2)), 99–110. Sendai: The 2005 SSM Research Committee.

IRES (2005), *Les Mutations de l'emploi*, Coll. Repère, Paris: La Découverte.

IRES (2009), *La France du travail*, Paris: Editions de l'Atelier.
Ishida, H. (2008), "Sedaikan idō e no seizon bunseki apurōchi (Survival analysis of intergenerational mobility)," in T. Watanabe (ed.), *Sedaikan idō to sedainai idō (2005-nen SSM chōsa shirīzu 3)* (Intergenerational and intragenerational mobility (The 2005 SSM research series; 3)), 55–74, Sendai: The 2005 SSM Research Committee.
Ishida, H. and D. H. Slater (2010), "Social class in Japan," in H. Ishida and D. H. Slater (eds), *Social class in contemporary Japan: Structures, sorting and strategies*, 1–29, London and New York: Routledge.
Iwai, H. (2008), "Sengo Nihon gata raifukōsu no jizoku to henyō (II): Josei no gakureki to raifukōsu no bunseki (Stability and change in the post-war Japanese life course (part 2): An analysis of women's education and life course)," in M. Nakai and I. Sugino (eds), *Raifukōsu-raifusutairu kara mita shakai kaisō (2005-nen SSM chōsa shirīzu 9)* (Social stratification from life course and lifestyle perspective (The 2005 SSM research series; 9)), 75–99, Sendai: The 2005 SSM Research Committee.
Kalleberg, A. L. and J. R. Lincoln (1988), "The structure of earnings inequality in the United States and Japan," *American Journal of Sociology*, 94: 121–153.
Kanbayashi, H. (2008), "Tenshoku-rishoku riyū no jidaiteki henka: Kōdo keizai seichōki kara 2005-nen made no sobyō (Longitudinal change of reasons for job changes and job quits in Japan: A description from 1956 to 2005)," in K. Agata (ed.), *Hatarakikata to kyaria keisei (2005-nen SSM chōsa shirīzu 4)* (Work style and career formation (The 2005 SSM research series; 4)), 67–84. Sendai: The 2005 SSM Research Committee.
Kanomata, N. (2008), "Baburu hōkai go no shotoku kakusa to shakai kaisō (Income differentials and social stratification after the collapse of the bubble economy)," in Yoshimichi Sato (ed.), *Ryūdōsei to kakusa no kaisōron (2005-nen SSM chōsa shirīzu 15)* (Disparities, social fluidity, and social stratification (The 2005 SSM research series; 15)), 47–65, Sendai: The 2005 SSM Research Committee.
Kariya, T. (1991), *Gakkō-shokugyō-senbatsu no shakaigaku. Kōsotsu shūshoku no Nihon-teki mekanizumu* (Sociology of schools, vocations, and selections: The Japanese mechanism of high school graduates' transition from school to work), Tokyo: Tokyo Daigaku Shuppankai.
Kitagawa, Y. (2005), "Tanshin dansei no hinkon to haijo (Exclusion and poverty of single men)" in M. Iwata and A. Nishizawa (eds), *Hinkon to shakaiteki-haijo* (Poverty and social exclusion), Tokyo: Mineruva Shobō, 223–227.
Kosugi, R. (2003), *Furītāā to iu ikikata* (Freeter as a lifestyle), Tokyo: Keisō Shobō.
Kosugi, R. (ed.) (2002), *Jiyū no daishō / furīta: Gendai wakamono no shūgyō ishiki to kōdō* (Freeters and the price of freedom: Employment awareness and behavior of contemporary youths), Tokyo: Nihon Rōdō Kenkyū Kikō.
La Mardière, C. de (1999), "Retour sur la valeur juridique de la Déclaration de 1789," *Revue française de droit constitutionnel*, 38: 227–256.
Langford, M. (ed.) (2009), *Socio-economic rights jurisprudence: Emerging trends in international and comparative law*, Cambridge: Cambridge University Press.

Leschke, J. and A. Watt (2008), *Job quality in Europe*, Working paper, 2008/07, ETUI.
Loison, M. (2007), "The Implementation of an Enforceable Right to Housing in France," *European Journal of Homelessness* 1, pp. 185–197.
Maruani, M. (2003), *Travail et emploi des Femmes*, Coll. Repère, Paris: La Découverte.
Maurin, E. (2005), *Le Ghetto Français*, La République des Idées, Paris: Le Seuil.
Maurin, E. (2009), *La Peur du Déclassement,* La République des Idées, Paris: Le Seuil.
Melucci, A. (1996), *The Playing Self: Person and Meaning in the Planetary Society*, Cambridge: Cambridge University Press.
Meunier, L. (2006), "Logement: la voie écossaise?," in *Alternatives économiques*, No. 248: available at http://www.alternatives-economiques.fr/page.php?controller=article&action=htmlimpression&id_article=23434&id_parution=201
Morita, Y. (2001), *Rakusō* (La classe déchue), Osaka: Nikei Osaka PR Kikaku shuppambu.
Mouchard, D. (2002), "Les mobilisations des 'sans' dans la France contemporaine: L'émergence d'un 'radicalisme autolimité'?," *Revue Française de Science Politique*, 52(4): 425–47.
Nagamatsu, N. (2008), "Shokugyō ni yoru shotoku kōzō no henka: Kyōsōteki sekutā ni okeru chūkansō no shotoku rekka (The change of the structure of earnings inequality by occupation: Earnings decrease of middle class in competitive industrial sector)," in Y. Sato (ed.), *Ryūdōsei to kakusa no kaisōron (2005-nen SSM chōsa shirīzu 15)* (Disparities, social fluidity, and social stratification (The 2005 SSM research series; 15)), 21–46, Sendai: The 2005 SSM Research Committee.
Nakazawa, W. (2008), "Jakunen rōdōshijō no ryūdōka to wa: Seizon bunseki apurōchi kara (What is the fluidity of the youth labor market in Japan? Based on survival analysis approaches)," in Y. Sato (ed.), *Ryūdōsei to kakusa no kaisōron (2005-nen SSM chōsa shirīzu 15)* (Disparities, social fluidity, and social stratification (The 2005 SSM research series; 15)), 113–131, Sendai: The 2005 SSM Research Committee.
Nolan, A., B. Thiele and M. Langford (2005), "Leading Cases on Economic, Social and Cultural Rights: Summaries—Working Paper No.2" (Geneva; COHRE), available at www.cohre.org
Nomura, M. (1994), *Shūshin kōyō* (Life-time employment), Tokyo: Iwanami Shoten.
Odaka, K. (1984), *Rōdō shijō bunseki: Nijū kōzō no Nihonteki tenkai* (An analysis of the labor market: Japanese development of the dual structure), Tokyo: Iwanami Shoten.
OECD (2007), *PISA 2006: Science Competencies for Tomorrow's World*, Paris: OECD.
OECD (2009), *Jobs for youth: Japan*, Paris: OECD.
Okba, M. and Lainé, F. (2004), "Les jeunes des zones sensibles et leurs difficultés d'insertion professionnelle, Annexe au Rapport au Conseil d'Analyse Economique intitulé," in J. P Fitoussi, E. Laurent and J.

Maurice, *Ségrégation urbaine et intégration sociale*, 279–295, Paris: La Documentation française.
Parsons, T. (1940), "An analytical approach to the theory of social stratification," *American Journal of Sociology*, 45(6): 841–862.
Paugam, S. (1991), *La disqualification sociale. Essai sur la nouvelle pauvreté*, Paris: PUF, 4ème édition "Quadrige," 2009.
Paugam, S. (2008), *Le lien social*, Coll. Que sais-je?, Paris: PUF
Paugam, S. (dir.) (1996), *L'exclusion, l'état des savoirs*, Paris: La Découverte.
Paugam, S. (2000) *Le salarié de la précarité. Les nouvelles formes de l'intégration professionnelle*, Coll. Le lien Social Paris: PUF, réédition "Quadrige" 2007 (avec une nouvelle préface).
Pekkanen, R. (2006), *Japan's Dual Civil Society, Members without Advocates*, Stanford: Stanford University Press.
Piore, M. J. and P. Doeringer (1971), *Internal Labor Markets and Manpower Adjustment*. New York: D.C. Heath and Company.
Porter, B. (2004), "Homelessness, Human Rights, Litigation and Law Reform: A View from Canada," *Australian Journal for Human Rights*, 10(2): 133–165.
Rémy, V. (2005), "Eléments de bilan sur les travaux évaluant l'efficacité des allègements de cotisations sociales employeurs," *Documents d'études de la DARES*, 101, juillet.
Rivero, J. (1990), "Déclarations parallèles et nouveaux droits de l'homme," *Revue trimestrielle des droits de l'homme*, 4: 323–329.
Rivero, J. (2003), *Libertés publiques*, Paris: PUF.
Roman, D. (2002), *Le droit face à la pauvreté*, Paris: L.G.D.J.
Roman, D. (2009), "Les droits sociaux, entre 'injusticiabilité' et 'conditionnalité': éléments pour une comparaison," *Revue internationale de droit comparé*, 2: 285–314.
Roman, D. (ed.) (2011) "Droits des pauvres, pauvres droits? Recherche sur la justiciabilité des droits sociaux," http://droits-sociaux.u-paris10.fr/index.php?id=40 (for the listed publications and collected resources).
Rosen, S. (1974), "Hedonic Prices and Implicit Markets: Product Differentiation in Pure Competition," *Journal of Political Economy*, 8: 35–55.
Sato, K. (2008), "Jakunensō no raifuchansu ni okeru hiseikikoyō no eikyō (Non-regular employment of youth and their life chances: Focusing on jobs and marriage)," in H. Tarohmaru (ed.), *Jakunensō no shakai idō to kaisōka (2005-nen SSM chōsa shirīzu 11)* (Social stratification and social mobility of young Japanese (The 2005 SSM research series; 11)), 67–79, Sendai: The 2005 SSM Research Committee.
Sato, Y. (2008), "Disparity society theory and social stratification theory: An attempt to respond to challenges by disparity society theory," in Y. Sato (ed.), *Ryūdōsei to kakusa no kaisōron (2005-nen SSM chōsa shirīzu 15)* (Disparities, social fluidity, and social stratification (The 2005 SSM research series; 15)), 1–20, Sendai: The 2005 SSM Research Committee.
Sato, Y. (2010), "Stability and increasing fluidity in the contemporary Japanese social stratification system," *Contemporary Japan*, 22: 7–21.
Sato, Y. and S. Arita (2008), "Globalization, local institutions, and middle classes: A comparative study of social mobility of middle classes in Japan and Korea," in S. Arita (ed.), *Higashi Ajia no kaisō dainamikkusu (2005-nen*

SSM chōsa shirīzu 13) (Dynamics of social stratification in East Asia (The 2005 SSM research series; 13)), 43–54, Sendai: The 2005 SSM Research Committee.

Schnapper D. (1981), *L'épreuve du chômage*, Paris: Gallimard (nouvelle édition; Coll. Folio, 1994).

Schnapper D. (avec la collaboration de Christian Bachelier) (2000), *Qu'est-ce que la citoyenneté?* Coll Folio, Paris: Gallimard .

Shinjuku Renraku Kai (1995), "Shinjuku Homeless 1995," *Shinjuku nojuku rōdōsha no genkyō to undo no kiroku* (Situation of workers living on the streets in Shinjuku and memories of their social movement), (unpublished).

Simmel, G. (1908), *Sociologie. Études sur les formes de la socialisation*, Paris: PUF.

Singly, F. de (2003), *Les uns avec les autres. Quand l'individualisme crée du lien*, Paris: Armand Colin.

Smith, A. (1776), *La Richesse des Nations*, réédition 1991, Paris: Flammarion.

Snow, D. (1993), *Down on Their Luck: A Study of Homeless Street People*, Berkeley: University of California Press.

Squires, J., M. Langford and B. Thiele (2005), *Road to a Remedy: Current Issues in Litigation of Economic, Social and Cultural Rights*, Sydney: Australian Human Rights Center and University of NSW Press

Takenoshita, H. (2008), "Labor market and job shift patterns in Japan: Voluntary and involuntary job mobility," in T. Watanabe (ed.), *Sedaikan idō to sedainaiidō (2005-nen SSM chōsa shirīzu 3)* (Intergenerational mobility and intragenerational mobility (The 2005 SSM research series; 3)), 161–186, Sendai: The 2005 SSM Research Committee.

Thiele, B. and M. Langford (eds) (2005), *Litigation of economic, social and cultural rights: The state of play*, Sydney: University of New South Wales Press.

Tomuschat, C. (2005), "An optional protocol for the international covenant on economic, social and cultural rights?," in *Weltinnenrecht. Liber amicorum Jost Delbrück*, 815–834, Berlin: Duncker and Humblot.

Touraine, A. (1991), "Face à l'exclusion," in J. Baudrillard et al. (eds), *Citoyenneté et Urbanité*, Paris: Esprit.

Tsutsumi, K. (2004), "The homeless issue and citizens: What was shown and what was hidden in the course of an incident, the case of Nagai Park Problem," *The Annuals of Sociological Association,* Osaka City University, Shidai Shakaigaku, 5: 29–36.

Yoshida, T. (2008a)," Shotoku tassei ni taisuru jakunenki kyaria no kōka (Young period job mobility and its consequences to income attainment)," in Y. Sato (ed.), *Ryūdōsei to kakusa no kaisōron (2005-nen SSM chōsa shirīzu 15)* (Disparities, social fluidity, and social stratification (The 2005 SSM research series; 15)), 99–112, Sendai: The 2005 SSM Research Committee.

Yoshida, T. (2008b), "Sedaikan shotoku idō kara mita kikai fubyōdō (Inequality of opportunity from a perspective of intergenerational income mobility)," in T. Watanabe (ed.), *Sedaikanidō to sedainaiidō (2005-nen SSM chōsa shirīzu 3)* (Intergenerational mobility and intragenerational mobility (The 2005 SSM research series; 3)), 147–160, Sendai: The 2005 SSM Research Committee.

Index

2005 Social Stratification and Mobility Survey (2005 SSM Project) 9–10, 17–18
AC! (*AgirEnsemble contre le Chômage!*) 102–3, 105–6, 108, 114, 145
Active Solidarity Income (RSA) 50, 84, 116, 119–23, 147
adjudicative space 129
associations 4, 77–8, 80–1, 83–4, 98, 139
Avenell, S. 87

blanket recruitment of new graduates 62, 69

citizenship link 22, 24–5, 27–8, 30–1
civil and political rights 130–2, 142, 148
civil rights 25
civil society 86–7, 97–101, 111, 140
CMU *see* Universal Health Cover
cultural rights 130–2, 142

DAL 102–3, 105–9, 113–14, 146
DALO 62, 139, 141, 150
degraded job 50, 52–6, 61
discrimination 1, 3–5, 28, 31, 55, 136, 145, 148–9

disincentive effects 120–1, 126
Droit au Logement *see* DAL
Droit au Logement Opposable *see* DALO
dualism 44, 62–3, 66, 73
Durkheim, E. 22, 24, 27

economic rights 131–6, 141–2, 148
elective participation link 22–8, 31
employment policies 116–20, 122–5, 127
employment subsidies 122
European March 103, 146
eviction 86–97, 114, 136, 140, 149

filiation link 27–8
freeter 10–11, 62, 64, 67, 106, 110, 112
French Constitution 130–1, 138, 147
French law 129–31
fundamental rights 25, 75, 78, 129, 131–2, 138, 143
furusato (native place) tax 42

gender 11, 50, 54–5, 101
globalization 8, 62, 69
Granovetter, M. 41

have-nots movement 103–7, 110–15

hikikomori (socially withdrawn people) 32, 68
homeless 30, 40, 65, 75, 79, 81–2, 84–109, 111–13, 139–40, 145–6
 movement 102–3, 108–9, 111–12
Homeless Rescue Service 81–2
human rights 25, 130–2, 134–6, 138, 142, 145, 148–50

ICESCR *see* International Covenant on Economic, Social and Cultural Rights
immigration 50
income inequality 9, 17–18
increasing fluidity 8
individual 1–6, 19, 21–7, 30–1, 34, 40, 45, 51, 53, 63, 74, 78, 85, 89, 100, 103–4, 110, 113–14, 118, 120, 130, 132, 147
International Covenant on Economic, Social and Cultural Rights 133–5, 148
inequality 2, 3, 9, 12, 17–18, 45–8, 52, 57, 87, 100, 134, 144

Japan/Japanese 8–13, 19, 32, 34–43, 62–4, 67–71, 73–4, 86–8, 91–3, 95, 98–112, 114, 144–6
job changes 9, 14–18
job quality 44, 46, 50–3, 55, 58
justiciability 130–5, 137–9, 141–3

labor cost 69, 116, 119–20, 122–3, 144

legal remedy 132
Lehman Shock 39
low wage 4, 66, 118–21, 123–6
 trap 125–6

mechanical solidarity 22
mental illness 36, 67
meritocracy 104, 146
middle class 67, 103–4, 110, 112
migrants 48, 92, 104, 106, 109
minimum income 79, 84, 108–19, 121–2, 126, 147
Minimum Insertion Income 75–7, 79, 84, 121–2, 126, 147
minimum wage 1, 105, 107, 110, 114, 120–4, 127, 147

NEET (Not in Education, employment or Training) 11, 32–7, 39, 42, 62, 67–8, 144
new social contract 130
NIMBY 87, 94, 100
non-regular worker 9, 13–15, 17–19, 62–6, 69, 72–3
NoVox 103, 145–6
NPO 35, 42, 87, 98, 100, 145

opposable rights 145
organic participation link 22, 24–31
organic solidarity 22, 24

part time jobs 124
Pekkanen, R. 87
Political rights 25, 130–2, 142, 148
politicization 86–7, 98
poor workers 75, 83
poverty 21, 29, 31–2, 36–7, 50, 63, 75–8, 84–5, 87, 100–1,

104, 106, 109, 111, 125–7, 129, 136, 143, 145, 149
reproduction of 36–7
trap 125–6
professional insertion 45, 77
protection 3, 14, 22–8, 31, 51, 64, 76–7, 84, 88–9, 106, 109, 120, 127–8, 130–2, 136, 139, 146, 149
public policies 75, 78, 81, 83, 86, 138
public vocational training 63

qualification 47, 49–50, 55

recognition 3, 20, 22–9, 31, 37, 57, 61, 84, 97–8, 130, 137, 139, 146
rent 19, 65, 106, 111, 113
resignation 33
RMI *see* Minimum Insertion Income

self-employed 38–9
shelterless populations 75
Simmel, G. 31
social classes 2–5, 8, 41–2
social contributions 80, 117–20, 122–3, 146–7
social exclusion 20, 32–4, 37, 39, 39–43, 75–7, 85, 85, 102, 104–6, 116
social forum 103, 145–6
Social hope 30
social housing 79–80, 140
social justice 1–5
social links 20–3, 25–9, 31
social minima 75, 78, 84
social movement 5, 102–6, 109–11, 114, 146

social movements 102, 104–5, 146
social protection 3, 24, 76–7, 84, 127–8
social rights 25, 27–8, 75–6, 129–38, 141–3, 148
Social Sciences of Hope 34
social security system 76, 83
social status 22, 25, 29
socio-economic rights 131
stability 8–9, 11, 14, 17, 19, 49, 51–2, 144
suicide 34–5

tax credit 118–19, 126
temporary employees 9, 40
temporary work 39–40, 49, 63, 106–7, 124
Tokyo 35, 86–8, 92, 95, 98–100, 102–3, 108, 113, 144–6
Totsuka Yacht School 39
town policy 80
transition from school to work 9

unemployment 2, 10, 16, 28–9, 45–50, 56, 76–7, 102–4, 114, 116–20, 122, 124–7, 147
Universal Declaration of Human Rights 25, 131–2, 135, 145
Universal Health Cover 81

vocational relevance of education 72–3

weak ties 41–2
welfare state 2, 7, 100
workfare 122

working class 47–8, 67
working conditions 15–6, 44, 51–3, 55–6, 59, 62–3, 66, 69–70, 73, 145
working poor 11, 119, 124

young people 10–12, 32, 36–7, 40, 42, 44–50, 53, 55–7, 62–4, 66–70, 73, 80, 106, 108, 112, 115, 117–19, 144
young workers 9, 11, 14, 16, 18, 63, 66–7, 69, 73, 118
youth labor market 14, 62–3, 66, 68, 73